SO YOU WANT TO BE AN ACTOR?

Prunella Scales
and Timothy West

NICK HERN BOOKS
London
www.nickhernbooks.co.uk

A NICK HERN BOOK

SO YOU WANT TO BE AN ACTOR?
first published in Great Britain in 2005
as a paperback original by Nick Hern Books Ltd,
The Glasshouse, 49a Goldhawk Road, London
W12 8QP

Reprinted 2006, 2007, 2008, 2010, 2012
Reprinted with revisions 2014, 2016

Cover Design by Peter Bennett
Cover Photo by Jane Bown

Typeset by Country Setting,
Kingsdown, Kent CT14 8ES
Printed and bound in Great Britain
by Ashford Colour Press Ltd, Gosport, Hants

British Library Cataloguing Data for this book
is available from the British Library

ISBN   978 1 85459 879 0

MIX
Paper from
responsible sources
FSC
www.fsc.org   FSC® C011748

TIMOTH

Among many stage performances, he may be

Beecham (Apollo, 1980), Josef Stalin in *Master
Class* (Wyndham's, 1984) and Lear in *King Lear*
(Old Vic, 2003); and on television in *Edward VII,
Churchill and the Generals, The Monocled
Mutineer* and *Brass*. He has taken part in over
500 radio broadcasts and recorded many Talking
Books. He was made CBE in 1984, holds
Honorary Doctorates at six British universities, is
currently President of the London Academy of
Music and Dramatic Art and of the Society for
Theatre Research. His autobiography, *A Moment
Towards The End Of The Play*, is published by
Nick Hern Books.

PRUNELLA SCALES

Prunella trained at the Old Vic Theatre School,
London, and with Uta Hagen in New York. She
has performed in seasons at Stratford-upon-Avon,
Chichester and the West Yorkshire Playhouse, as
well as at the National Theatre. London
appearances also include *Hay Fever, When We Are
Married, Quartermaine's Terms, Single Spies* and
A Day In The Death Of Joe Egg. On television,
she is remembered for the series *Fawlty Towers,
After Henry* and *Mapp and Lucia*, as well as the
dramas, *Signs and Wonders, The Rector's Wife*
and *Breaking the Code. An Evening With Queen
Victoria*, a portrait of the monarch in her own
words, in which Prunella is joined by two
musicians, has been performed all round the
world on an occasional basis for twenty-five years.

Timothy West and Prunella Scales have been
married since 1963 and have frequently
appeared on stage together. They have two sons,
one of whom, Samuel West, has followed them
into the profession.

IN THE SAME SERIES

ALSO BY TIMOTHY WEST

For the aspiring performer, there is no such thing as an absolute rulebook, no reliable common counsel. No two actors think alike, so what the undersigned pair have to say may often be mutually contradictory. Some of the advice may be bad. Some of it, on the other hand, may be so good that we wish we had taken it ourselves. But at least it has no pretence to canon law – it's simply a set of individual opinions born of an aggregate of a hundred years in the business.

Prunella Scales
Timothy West

Contents

PREPARATION

PRACTICE

PERSEVERANCE

APPENDIX

NOTE

As you will see, the two authors alternate throughout the book, distinguished one from the other by different typefaces.

This is Prunella Scales's 'voice'.

And this is Timothy West's 'voice'.

I

PREPARATION

FIRST THOUGHTS ABOUT
BECOMING AN ACTOR

What gave you the idea? Did you go to the theatre much as a child? The cinema? Watch a lot of drama on TV, and wish you were doing it? Did you do many plays at school, or with amateur groups, and found you liked it, or were quite good?

All these are perfectly valid reasons for trying to go into the business. But above all, don't do it as Second Best.

We will not insult the obvious intelligence you have displayed in buying this book by supposing that you believe the life of an actor is one long round of companionable jollity, a passport to fame, fortune, free sex and fashionable restaurants. It could be that you hold a more pragmatic view of your likely development: starting as a badly paid, unknown and unappreciated small-part player in some far-flung theatre never visited by casting directors, gradually getting better parts, achieving a modest foothold in television, developing by sheer hard work into someone who might one day be employed by the National Theatre or the RSC.

That sounds logical, but I'm afraid it very seldom works like that. No, your development will largely depend on luck, fashion, who you know, what you look like, and the general state of the business. It's tough, but there it is. HOWEVER, before you cast this book away in despair – talent comes into it somewhere. So does your ability to work hard and variously, and to be easy to get along with.

Think very hard about it. Unemployment statistics in the profession are hard to ascertain accurately, but a recent Equity survey showed that only some 56 per cent of members earned less than £10,000 a year from performing, while around 35 per cent worked fewer than 10 weeks. Of course, that's only *Equity members* (more about that later), and, among them, only those who responded to the survey.

If you honestly feel that you will have difficulty coping with lengthy periods of hardship and frustration, then you should seriously consider the alternative option of taking what my father (who worked in the theatre all his life) used to call a Proper Job. Then you can join one of the better amateur companies and carry on acting in your spare time. This is what I did, when I tried for a time to do a Proper Job. So what went wrong, you ask? Well, I simply found that my after-hours dramatic activity was eating up most of my energy, enthusiasm and, indeed, thought. So it seemed reasonable to try and get paid (modestly) for what I clearly cared about most.

The British actress Athene Seyler, in her book *The Craft of Comedy* (get it, if you haven't got it), refers to an imaginary friend making the leap from amateur to professional theatre: 'William . . . is marrying his mistress, as it were, and what has up till now been simply delight in the expression of his love for her, will turn into staid responsibility and monotony, with all the other cares attendant upon married life.'

HOW TO GO ABOUT IT

The best advice I could give a young person wanting to be an actor is, 'Finish your education.' Don't go to a Child Acting School, but get as broad an education as you can, and don't do 'Drama' as an academic subject. A professional actor doesn't need to know about Drama, but about Life. You need to observe and understand 'real' people. If you go on to university, read English, History, Music, a foreign language, or even a scientific subject. Do as much acting as you can in your free time or out of school and university hours. An actor has to understand the circumstances and mind-set of every character he plays, so the fuller his experience and knowledge of people, the better.

If you plan to allow yourself a 'gap year' between school and university, this could well be used as an opportunity to broaden your knowledge of life and society, and to learn more about the sort of characters you hope to play as an actor. Get a job where you meet lots of different people, and which ideally gives you the chance to save some money for the future.

I have an ambivalent attitude to the study of Drama at university level. The late Professor Glynne Wickham, who founded the first-ever Drama Department at a British University (Bristol), used to greet his new students by telling them that if they had any idea of becoming actors then they shouldn't be there at all – they should be getting vocational training up the road at the Bristol Old Vic Theatre School. His own Department was, he maintained, properly for the use of academics, writers, artistic directors, theatrical historians, dramaturgs and critics.

Wickham, who knew perfectly well that many of his students *would* go on to become actors, was being very shrewd. Among the alumni of his time at Bristol are in fact some of the most distinguished figures in our business. That distinction could well be due to their having been able to share their early adult life with students of every kind of subject: yes, 'real' people.

TO TRAIN OR NOT TO TRAIN

Forty years ago, the shrinking number of repertory theatres in this country still offered a core of actors continuous employment throughout a season, or perhaps a whole year, sometimes even longer. People starting their careers in one of the better Reps therefore had the opportunity to cut their teeth on the language of Shakespeare, Congreve, Sheridan, Wilde, Shaw, Coward, Rattigan and Agatha Christie, as well as translations of Chekhov, Ibsen and

Molière. But learning the job just by doing it is no longer a real option, and only enrolment at a Drama School can provide some measure of that varied experience.

Drama Schools nowadays provide full tuition in performing before the camera and the microphone as well as on stage. However, there is a feeling among some senior television producers today that drama training of any kind works against the colloquial naturalism demanded for popular 'soaps', and that actors for such programmes are better recruited directly off the street.

This is fine, if you are prepared to go on doing that sort of thing for the rest of your life (or until the producers get bored with you), but if you later feel a thirst to explore different kinds of writing, perhaps in the live theatre, you could find yourself in difficulties given the vocal and physical scale, along with the stamina and preparation necessary to sustain a performance over two and a half hours.

This can only be learned by practice, and you may wish you'd gone to Drama School after all.

I didn't go to Drama School, but Pru did.

It was the remarkable, though short-lived, Old Vic Theatre School in London, run by Michel Saint-Denis, George Devine and Glen Byam Shaw. At the age of seventeen and two months, with my very thick glasses and pigtails, I didn't have a very good time there, but the training itself, based on Stanislavski, was illuminated for me some years later at The Herbert Berghof Studio in New York, run by the brilliant actress and teacher, Uta Hagen – more of this later.

At the Old Vic School, the teaching of Litz Pisk was revelatory, and I believe her book *The Actor and His Body* to be essential reading for all aspiring actors. In working with us on period dances, Litz would draw parallels between the costume, architecture and social attitudes of different ages. Two examples that have stayed in mind are: the correlation between the mediæval aspiration to Heaven echoed in both Gothic architecture and the vertical pointed 'hennin' worn by women on their heads, and the sexual hypocrisy of the Edwardian age as reflected in the mens' stiff collars and the women's high-buttoned jackets, over-emphasised breasts and exaggerated 'bustles' – the scaled-down remnant of the Victorian crinoline – sticking out behind.

DRAMA SCHOOL

In the relevant section of *Contacts* – (published annually by The Spotlight; get a copy if you haven't one already) – Drama UK (formed from a merger of the Conference of Drama Schools and the National Conference of Drama Training) represents twenty nationwide drama schools. The list is reprinted at the end of this book. These are the leading schools of the country, offering accredited courses, most of which are now accorded degree status.

Obtaining funding to go to Drama School is easier than it used to be, although the funding system itself is more complicated.

Three schools – RADA, LAMDA and Bristol Old Vic Theatre School – are part of the National Conservatoire of Dance & Drama. If you get into one of these you may apply for a scholarship to aid with your tuition fees.

Almost all other Drama Schools are associated with Universities or Colleges of Higher Education. They offer degree-level courses. Consequently, students are eligible to apply for student loans.

Six schools – ALRA, Arts Ed, Guildford School of Acting (Acting course only), Italia Conti Academy of Theatre Arts, Mountview Academy of Theatre Arts and Oxford School of Drama – offer Dance and Drama Awards to selected students. D&DAs are scholarships provided by the government to allow 'the most talented' students to attend independent Drama Schools. The D&DAs are usually offered to students who would benefit from training but who wouldn't be able to pay the fees. The D&DA scheme, therefore, makes access easier, although you can't apply for help with living costs if your combined parental income is more than £30,000 a year (this was the figure in 2014/2015 academic year). But you should ask, if you go to one of these schools as a fee-payer, whether you can apply for a student loan.

Cygnet Training Theatre in Exeter is completely independent, so if you go there you'll receive no public funding but may apply for a Professional and Career Development Loan.

Those schools are the training places responsible for turning out the vast majority of our leading performers.

Contacts then goes on to devote many pages to listing other organisations devoted to drama training, from fully-fledged schools to individual practitioners, speech therapists, dialect experts and the like.

Well, many of these institutions are entirely reputable, and a great number of the practising individuals offer expert and helpful guidance. Even so, so many retailers all laying out their wares for the budding trainee is rather confusing to say the least.

Choose carefully.

For some time I was on the Accreditation Panel of the National Council for Drama Training, and while I have seen some excellent teaching, and watched some excellent work over the years, I have to say – as a crazy idealist – that I'd like to see the number of accredited Drama Schools in the UK reduced to twelve: say six in London, and one each in Glasgow, Cardiff, Belfast, Birmingham, Manchester and Bristol. I feel there cannot possibly be enough really good teachers to spread the net much wider than this.

However, if you can get a place, and can spare the three years (or if you're a post-graduate, two years) required for an Accredited Drama Training, it's an opportunity to develop the skills you need for stage, screen and radio – a trained voice, singing, dance, fencing, gymnastics, learning various dialects, wearing of costume, make-up skills and so on.

Buy *Contacts*, study the list of schools, write to a few you like the look of and ask for a prospectus from each, or visit their website. Read this material carefully, and having done so, make a shortlist of three or four. If your application is granted, they'll tell you the sort of thing they will expect you to prepare for the audition, and will warn you that they charge a fee. At your interview they will want to be convinced of your commitment, your health and physical fitness, your willingness to learn and to work hard, and not least, your ability to cover your maintenance costs and, if applicable, tuition fees.

Don't expect to succeed on your first attempt. The demand to get into a reputable school gets fiercer all the time. (LAMDA, the one I know most about, takes only 3.5% of its annual applicants.) But let us suppose you've done your audition, had your interview, been accepted, had your funding guaranteed, signed your contract, and are now ready to start.

I hope you've managed to save a bit of money to tide you through your first year, because maintenance expenses, especially if you've hitherto lived out of London and are facing for the first time the cost of living in the capital, can be colossal. Many students try to solve this problem by working in bars, restaurants and cafés in the evenings and at weekends, but it's essential not to let this tire you out to the extent of being unable to concentrate on your classes in the morning, or to study your lines. Or indeed to go to the theatre to see the profession at work!

Learn to be frugal. Some students in their first term feel they have to impress their fellows by flashing the latest trainers, tracksuits and mobile telephones. Don't get drawn into this competition.

Instead, spend any spare money you have on useful books, visiting exhibitions and art galleries, going to concerts and the cinema – and especially to the theatre.

Many theatres have a policy of giving away unsold seats to students on the day of performance; others will let you in at student rates for considerably less than you'd spend in an average evening at a pub or club. Nevertheless, a surprising number of drama students never seem to go to the theatre at all. (Why is this? Music students go to hear musicians, art students go to look at pictures.) Perhaps they believe most professional theatre is rubbish? That's no excuse not to go – occasionally it's good to see something done badly so that you can see clearly how to do it better.

GRADUATION

During your last year at Drama School, productions will be attended by a number of agents, casting directors and the like. You may feel that the parts in which you are seen don't show you up to your best advantage or full potential, but don't worry about this. People understand the exigencies of Drama School casting, and will be more concerned about your sense of truth and general ability than whether you're the right age (you probably aren't) or physically suitable for the part.

A word of warning about those public performances. Your audience will normally be largely composed of your fellow students, and they, being the nice people they are, will be rooting for you, laughing delightedly at every funny thing you do or say. It's a great feeling, But just remember it's not going to be like that when you go into the business.

Most schools also present a programme of short scenes – usually duologues – to be performed by the graduating students over an afternoon in a West End theatre, to an audience of potential employers. Here, you will have more opportunity to choose parts for which you might perhaps reasonably be cast.

Be sensible about this. Once, at an audition, a tall and very thin young actor surprised me by giving a rendition of Falstaff's 'honour' speech just because, as he explained, he liked it.

Pick a piece that people are not going to know by heart – unless you have something mind-bogglingly original to say about it. The style in which it is written needs to be one in which you feel absolutely at home. Make sure that your excerpt works for itself, and doesn't need to be seen in the context of the entire play in order to be properly understood. The people out front might know the play quite well, however, and it will count against you if they suspect you haven't bothered to read it first. I am frequently shocked nowadays, when taking classes, or coaching people for auditions, that many young actors will prepare a speech or scene without having read the whole play. I believe this to be an artistic and professional sin. It's essential to research the character, the situation, the historical period and all the relationships in the play as exhaustively as possible, both before and during rehearsals: yes, OK, much or even most of your research may not be useful in the end, but you will at least have the knowledge that you've done it, and this can give added conviction and authority to your performance.

UNPAID FRINGE PRODUCTIONS

One way of putting yourself on the map – though at your own expense – is to create, devise or somehow bring about a performance, either alone or with a group of similarly-placed colleagues, and offer it to a Fringe venue. Don't try the established theatres like the Islington King's Head or the Finborough; there are lots of lesser-known places both in London and the regions which will, for a standard rental and if your show is any good at all, provide you with a space to play in for a week or more. After that, it is up to you to publicise the event and to solicit the attendance of any agents, producers, casting directors and other potential employers, and even members of the press that you think might be persuaded to come.

AGENTS

A number of agents attend final-year productions at Drama School and may follow up their visits with an offer of trial representation. Otherwise, the school will have a record of what agents have been to which shows, and will tell you whether they think it's worth your contacting them.

You may genuinely feel that you were miscast in your final showings, or that you weren't seen in anything flashy enough to attract attention; it's worth writing to those agents who were at least present at the performance, and asking if you may come and see them.

If you didn't go to Drama School, and have nobody to advise you, I'm afraid it's a question of looking down an immensely long list of agents (*Contacts* again) and writing a lot of letters/emails asking for an interview (don't phone). Mention anything you've been in, even at school, and send them a good photograph (see next section under Advertising Yourself). If you've been able to record yourself doing something, let them know, but don't send them a copy in the first instance, because you won't get it back. You won't get the photo back either; it's a costly business, I'm afraid, and you may well find you don't get any response at all.

Obviously it is a great advantage, although not absolutely essential, to provide yourself with an agent before you set out in the world. Agents know, or should know, what is going on in the business, what shows are being cast, what films are in preparation, what TV series are in production, and which casting directors are keen to know about new acting talent.

However, do not expect your agent to work miracles. He or she is in a competitive position with other agencies who are pushing their own clients. A lot of the work that comes your way – and this becomes truer as you get older – you may well have got by your own efforts, but it is still essential to have a third person to speak for you in negotiating contracts, salaries, billing and so on.

Remember that agents have to eat too, so don't be surprised if they lean on you sometimes to turn down that interesting new play in a Fringe theatre in the Midlands, and push you towards a commercial voice-over that will earn them a bigger commission. Agents used to take an agreed ten per cent of the client's earnings, nowadays it's often twelve-an-a-half, or fifteen even: their expenses are escalating, like yours.

A good agent, though, will always be considering what will be best for you in the long term. Neither Pru nor I are fond of the word 'career'; to me it suggests an unstoppable upward linear journey towards an ultimate goal; let's just say your future development as an actor will often mean looking beyond some immediately attractive proposition to focus on something that in the end may turn out to be of more lasting value.

ADVERTISING YOURSELF

You will need to get some good portrait photographs taken – preferably by a specialist theatre photographer – and have quite a lot of postcard-sized reproductions done of the two or three you like best, and which are recognisable when you present yourself at interviews.

Have a look through *Spotlight,* a huge directory of actors, either in print or online, in order to get the feeling of your colleagues' advertisements. Your Drama School will have the full collection, as should the larger Public Libraries. Some of the pictures will suggest the subject's partiality for a specific style of work: a girl with a bubbly blonde wig and a zany expression is probably telling you she doesn't expect to be considered for Medea, while a sombre, cadaverous, side-lit man braced against a brick wall is perhaps signalling his taste for TV psycho-thrillers. Look up an actor whose work you've seen and admired recently, and think whether, if you'd been in charge of casting, the photograph in front of you would have helped you make your choice. Ask yourself, too, whether it brings out the qualities that you specially valued about the performance you saw.

Have a session with a professional photographer – the work of amateurs will not do, however good you consider the results. There are a great many specialists in theatrical portrait photography: *Contacts* is full of their advertisements. Pick one whose work looks to you truthful, sympathetic, and, above all, accurate. Nothing is more irritating to a potential employer, when interviewing an actor, than the door opening to admit someone completely unrecognisable from the photo on the desk.

The *Spotlight* book requires photographs to be in black and white; your information will also be on their website. Select your own two shots from those shortlisted by your photographer, seek the advice of your agent about which finally to choose, then you can get an entry form from the *Spotlight* office, 7 Leicester Place, London WC2H 7RJ, fill in the details as required and return it, together with your chosen photographs, to which you must by law attach the name of the professional photographer. You can also acquire membership very easily through their website (www.spotlight.com/join).

Write (enclosing perhaps a different photograph) to the Artistic Directors of regional producing companies, Reps, as well as those in London, keeping your letters short but informative. Write also to Casting Directors (all these are listed in *Contacts*) and producers and directors of shows that you have seen on television or heard on radio. Bear in mind that in many cases nowadays directors do not have an absolute say in casting, the responsibility for which is now passing to Executive Producers, Commissioning Editors and other nabobs whom you will never meet. And don't be discouraged if you receive few, if any, answers to your letters: they'll be on a file somewhere, and may produce results at some later date.

AUDITIONS AND INTERVIEWS

How do you get an audition? If you don't have an agent, how do you find out where, when, and for what auditions are to be held? Write to the casting departments of major companies (such as the National Theatre or the Royal Shakespeare Company) to find out about how they cast their shows.

Information about auditions for specific projects, particularly in the commercial sector, is harder to obtain. Just occasionally advertisements appear in *The Stage* newspaper, and you can write to producers asking whether they are holding any auditions; but a lot of young actors rely on their agents or websites such as Casting Call Pro. One way is to write to theatre managements offering your services as an usher/ette. This will bring you into contact with people who know a bit about what is going on.

If you are offered an audition, find out about the venue in which it is to be held. It might be a comfortable 120-seater auditorium, or it might hold 2,000. If it's the latter, don't bother rehearsing in your bedroom, get out on to some unpopulated waste ground or a deserted car park, and check the scale and audibility of your performance with a friend.

When you get onto the stage, state your name and say what you're going to do, and just do it. If they want to talk to you, they'll usually do it afterwards. Introductory explanations about your chosen piece are not generally viewed kindly, nor are Lee Strasberg-style pauses for psychological preparation.

Of course, you may genuinely require time for preparation, but try to do it while you're waiting to be called to go on – as you would, indeed, during a live professional performance.

If you're going to sing, trust the accompanist who's been provided. They're normally old hands, at home equally with Schubert or Sondheim. Give them a clean piano part and let them get on with it; they'll follow you.

When you've come to read for a particular part, it's only sensible to wear something that will help to suggest the character. Years ago, when I was reading for the part of a village idiot, I turned up in stained corduroys and a moth-eaten sweater in competition with half-a-dozen other actors all wearing (as was the custom in those days) clean shirts and pressed trousers. I got the part before I'd opened my mouth.

When you are being interviewed for a job, it's important to give an impression of confidence without seeming pushy. In the United States, it is expected for you to sell yourself quite aggressively to potential employers: over here, we're less keen on the 'in your face' approach.

Nevertheless, you've got to be ready to answer sometimes quite personal questions about your background and achievements without reluctance or embarrassment. If you get the feeling that you may be turning out not to be quite what your interviewer envisaged, it is always worth asking to *read*. You could be doing both of you a favour.

SPREADING YOURSELF AROUND

The field of possible employment for an actor today is actually extraordinarily wide. Beyond the recognised areas of TV, film and radio there is the whole world of commercial advertising, presentation, voice-overs and a considerable Talking Books industry. In addition to conventional stage work, we have theatre-in-education, theatre-in-business, role-play companies, small-scale foreign touring, corporate entertaining, recitals and occasional opportunities to work alongside musicians, sportsmen and women, and circus performers.

I list these different possibilities simply as an encouragement; you won't find your way into most of them immediately. You can, however, find out about the educational work from theatre companies who offer this facility, or from your local government authority. Consider also working up a recital programme consisting of snippets from established writers on a particular subject, either for yourself or with a partner. Tim and I have compiled a number of such programmes, and they're a useful, portable and often lucrative reserve. Also it's a chance to be heard speaking some of the best writing in the English language, which ordinarily might not come your way.

Think, when you start out, as widely as you can. Your Drama School will have tried to train you for all eventualities, so take an early opportunity to explore as many different areas, and separate kinds of work, as may come your way. It makes a lot of sense to stretch your physical and mental muscles, learn new skills, build up a list of contacts for later, and earn a little money while you're doing it. And it's more interesting than sitting at home waiting for one day on *Holby City*.

FINANCIAL SECURITY

Learn a trade or acquire a skill that will earn you the rent when you are out of work. I have already referred to Equity figures showing what percentage of us are in work at any one time; unemployment is nothing to be ashamed of, it's simply sensible to have something else to fall back on.

Save, if you can, 25 per cent of your earnings against the possibility of your being presented with an unexpected tax demand.

I think 25 per cent is unreasonable, but by all means try!

If you are fortunate enough to land a job in a TV series, or a well-paid film, or a long run in the West End, the Tax Man will pounce, and you have to know how to deal with him. Get yourself a really good accountant – ask around while you're working, or Equity will usually recommend someone suitable – and form the habit early in your life of keeping all receipts: food, drink (this comes under 'entertaining and meals away from home'), travel (if you're rash enough to take a taxi, always ask for a receipt), medicines, wardrobe, make-up, research material, publications, theatre and cinema tickets, CDs, subscriptions to professional organisations, gymnasium expenses, hairdressing, and so on.
A certain proportion of these can be claimed against tax; and so can the accountant's fee. If you are able to maintain a savings account, then tax arrears, one of the potential nightmares of the business, can be avoided.

EQUITY

The British Actors' Equity Association represents actors, singers, dancers, choreographers, variety and circus artists, stage management, theatre designers and directors, TV and radio presenters, walk-on and supporting artists, stunt performers and fight arrangers. It is there to protect its members against increasing attempts within this business to destabilise fees and conditions, extend working hours and cut corners in a variety of other ways.

A few years ago Equity fought a long, complex and ultimately successful legal battle with the Inland Revenue to preserve Schedule D status for actors, without which it would have been impossible to make those claims against tax Pru has just talked about. More recently, their campaign to draw the Government's attention to the financial plight of regional theatres, and those working in them, resulted in a pay agreement bringing in over £1 million a year to the impoverished subsidised Reps. Current concerns include the re-establishment of tax-breaks for the British film industry, proper monitoring of TV repeat fees, controlling the practice of using amateurs on film locations, and positive discrimination in favour of women performers where appropriate.

Before Margaret Thatcher's assault on trades unions in the 1980s, Equity was a closed shop. You were given provisional membership when you graduated from Drama School, or started in rep as a working student. After forty weeks' work in Equity-controlled theatres, you qualified as a full member. If you had not achieved this, someone had to produce a very good reason indeed to employ you in the theatre or television. Since de-unionisation, membership has become non-mandatory, and although the bulk of employers adhere to Equity's legislation, in some places non-union members are happy to work below the minimum wage, and without the safety and insurance cover provided.

Do join. The organisation can do so much for you. Equity's advisory services provide information about insurance, pensions, legal and welfare, accountancy, lodgings, rights, royalties, provision of equipment and information about jobs.

There is no longer a required routine, or period of apprenticeship, for entry. 'Any person who exercises professional skill in the provision of entertainment, in accordance with criteria laid down from time to time by the (Equity) Council, shall be eligible for membership. The Council may, but shall not be obliged to, provide for special classes of membership, e.g. to take account of age and student status; to offer temporary membership; to provide for differing rates of entrance fees and subscriptions.' Graduates from a CDS school or CDET-accredited courses automatically qualify for membership, and there is a student membership scheme. There is a one-off joining fee of £28 (in 2014); subscription varies according to circumstance.

In an ideal world I would like Equity once again to be a post-entry closed shop. Membership would conventionally be by graduation from any of the accredited Drama Schools, but if for any reason an untrained actor is cast in a play, film or television series, he should go on to do a one-year course at one such school before continuing in the business. I believe strongly in the full unionisation of the profession, both to protect salary structures and limit unemployment. A vain belief, perhaps, but then there is room for a lot of crazy idealism in this business.

Crazy indeed, and obviously wholly impractical.

HEALTH

Look after your health; it's an important asset. Find yourself a good doctor, and a good dentist on the National Health if possible, and if possible stick with them during your working life (or theirs). If you do have to 'go private' for any special treatment, there's a good chance you can claim the expense against tax.

Although I believe passionately in a Socialist State with an efficient National Health Service for all, it is sensible for actors to have a modest private health insurance policy against emergencies and to avoid inconveniencing colleagues and employers by undue absences from rehearsals while waiting in National Health queues.

Take good care of your teeth: clean them after every meal and of course before you go to bed. Carry some strong mints with you every day, so that if you're rehearsing close to another actor your breath is nice to work with. If you're advised to have any cosmetic dentistry, go for it. Again, you can claim this against tax as a professional expense.

PHYSICAL WELL-BEING

It's a professional responsibility for an actor to keep fit, and not to let colleagues or management down through illness and absence, loss of voice, spreading colds and so on. It's also sensible not to get overweight (or anorexic) – any failure of health will be all round the business, especially potential employers, within days. If you're working in the live theatre there may be provision for a physical warm-up for the company before the 'half' is called, or you may like to do this on your own. I like anyway to get into the building at least an hour before curtain up so as to have a quick twenty minutes' kip before getting into costume, to deal with any messages or correspondence, and clean any wigs or whiskers not taken care of by the management. Vocally, too, it's good to warm up for a few minutes:

most managements allow you to do that on stage, but spare a thought for your colleagues who may be hearing you in their dressing rooms over the Tannoy.

READING MATTER

You will be leaving Drama School having absorbed a lot of acting theory, and probably come away with the view that the teaching of Stanislavsky all boils down to simple common sense. Two books, though, I'd regard as essential study if you haven't already found them: Uta Hagen's seminal *Respect for Acting,* and the really excellent *The End of Acting* by another American, Richard Hornby, which, as well as setting you on the right track, refreshingly debunks a whole lot of mistaken dogma.

But you can spend too much time on theory. Read plenty of plays, novels, poetry, and get a feeling for the different periods, styles, language in which they were written. Go through Shakespeare, Shaw, Wilde, Sheridan when you're out of work, and modern writers too of course; it'll equip you to cope better with the text when you come to deal with them in practice.

If you need a particular book, and can't afford it, go to a public library. Down-loading little bits of plays or novels from the Internet is fiddly and unsatisfactory.

If I had my life over again, I think one of the rules I would set myself is to acquire *only* books of reference – though the books of reference an actor should have ready to hand would fill a small flat – dictionaries of course, English, French, Spanish, Italian and German, history books and encyclopedias.

Our own shelves are bursting with these volumes, but outnumbered by yards and yards of much-loved other literature and quite a lot of, let's face it, rubbish, which we haven't the energy or will-power to take down to the charity shop.

ONWARD . . .

So let us assume you have now made the transition from valued and fully-qualified drama student to itinerant job-seeking actor. You will for a while miss the security and companionship, but cheer up. Once you get started, you will begin to feel part of a generous and supportive family, a resource to draw on for sympathy and encouragement. With a very few notable – and noted – exceptions, actors are nice people.

One more word from Athene Seyler:

'Give William my best wishes; not for success, but for achievement. He will mix the two up in his mind for some years, but if he is an artist, he will distinguish between them in time.'

II

PRACTICE

WHAT IS ACTING FOR?

The purpose of acting is, or should be, to deliver what the author has written to the audience who have paid – or switched on their TV – that night. There is a wonderful letter from George Bernard Shaw written to the actress Janet Achurch when she was about to play his Candida in New York:

'Observe, Janet Achurch, what you have to do is *play the part*. You have not to make a success. New York must notice nothing: it must say "Of course," and go home quietly. If it says "Hooray," then you will be a mere popular actress, a sort of person whom I utterly decline to know.'

I believe acting to be primarily an interpretative job – or art, if you're lucky – not necessarily a creative one, although of course a great deal of creative talent and energy can go into it. Indeed, with less than satisfactory writing, a good deal of creativity will be *necessary*, both from director and actors. But in ideal circumstances, with really good material, the job of the director and cast is to serve that material – to serve it up, if you like, perfectly prepared, well flavoured, at the appropriate temperature, and leaving them gasping for more.

Really good plays are a privilege to do, and should be so regarded. Most of our lives are spent making average work seem good, poor work seem average, and really terrible work seem bearable.

APPROACH TO A CHARACTER

In an ideal world, and given adequate time, I believe an actor should ask the following questions of himself:

First, Who am I? (CHARACTER).

Second, What do I want? (OBJECTIVE).

Third, What are the *circumstances* – physical and non-physical?

Fourth, What are the *obstacles*, physical and non-physical?

And finally, given all of the above: What do I *do*? (ACTION).

In other words, don't play qualities or emotions, play what you *do about them*.

TRUTH

This is the term we use to define *credibility* in what we do. A truthful way of playing a situation, or speaking a line, or responding to one, will be the result of your chosen thought at that moment. The audience doesn't need to know *why* you were thinking that thought at that precise moment, but as long as you came to it through some psychological route that makes sense to *you*, within your character and situation, they'll believe it.

When I'm rehearsing, I try to draw a thought-line through the whole part from beginning to end, so that I know pretty well what my character is thinking at every moment of the play. At night, I read through the play and ask myself (a) whether this bears the weight of *truth*. If I'm persuaded it does, I read it again to decide (b) whether what I'm intending to do will be *clear* to the audience. It's no good being ever so truthful if people can't follow what you're doing. Finally, if the answer's yes, it's time to enquire (c) will it be *interesting*? Useless being truthful and crystal clear if what you've come up with is really boring.

These three questions need to be asked, *in that order.*

TECHNICAL ADVICE — SHAPE

Think about the shape you make on the stage – or the screen. First, of course, make sure it's appropriate to the part, as interesting and entertaining as possible, without appearing self-indulgent. Secondly, however much in character your gestures are, don't let them become inappropriately repetitive – don't tire the audience's eyes with finger-wagging, or their ears with monotonous or repetitive inflections (unless it's on purpose, after consultation with the director).

Introducing some individual physical habit or repeated gesture into your performance may seem a neat way of getting your character into focus. However, don't fall too much in love with the idea. In Chichester, I once played the financially obsessive Dr Shpigelsky in Turgenev's *A Month in the Country*, and I had the notion of tapping the loose change in my pocket every time I offered another character some piece of self-interested advice. It made a nice noise, and the critics loved it; such a gesture, they said, spoke louder than a page of dialogue. For some reason, instead of feeling pleased, this made me rather cross; and when the production moved into the West End, I decided to think the same thought but without doing the gesture, and it was *better.*

USE OF LANGUAGE

I've always been somewhat obsessed with the sound of speech, and believe strongly that a feeling for language and how it is spoken can give you an insight into the psychology that produces it – there are a great many nerve endings round our vocal equipment, and by imitating a dialect or accent one can very often penetrate the physical and/or psychological make-up of the character. I grew up all over the place, and during my childhood and teens became proficient in several regional dialects: North Devon, where I went to primary school; Educated Welsh because the teacher was a Mrs Thomas; East End cockney because a crowd of evacuees arrived at the school in 1940; West Yorkshire because we stayed for a long time with our aunt outside Huddersfield, where I subsequently played in weekly rep; South London where I was a student; and East Coast American, where I was playing for five months in New York in the fifties.

While in New York I studied with Uta Hagen. She finally made clear for me the teaching of Stanislavsky as well as demystifying the rather daunting 'Method' approach of Lee Strasberg. Tim has already mentioned Uta's book *Respect for Acting*, and she's written another: *A Challenge for the Actor*.

Try to develop an ear and feeling for different *styles* of language – the language of different periods, different characters, different social classes and so on. Realise that the dramatist has deliberately chosen words and phrases or arranged them in a particular way which is apt for the character and the scene: it's our job as actors to *justify* the text, however unusual or eccentric, in a way that sounds like the character's natural way of expressing him or herself.

'R.P.'

R.P., or Received Pronunciation, is the term still used to describe reasonably educated speech spoken in England south of, say, Birmingham. But many now would ask, 'Received by whom?'

The sound of English speech has been changing constantly throughout history; and recently we've seen a rapid acceleration of that process, first apparent, as one would expect, among younger people. Breakdown of the class structure has produced the amalgam that has been termed Estuary English – rather inaccurate because it pretty well covers the whole southern half of England. Another thing that's happening to language is that southern upward-mobility, agricultural decline and relocation of employment are steadily jettisoning local words and ironing out regional speech differences. Television has of course exerted a strong influence on how people speak, and broadcasters are tending now to abandon authoritative R.P. for a more informal, chummy approach, employing news, weather and continuity presenters with either genuine regional or 'estuary' accents.

The most significant modern blow to English vowel-sounds, however, has been delivered from the other side of the globe. From the Australian TV soap *Neighbours* we have inherited the upward inflection at the end of a sentence, the tortuous diphthong 'nouyiw' for 'no', and the almost complete loss of the traditional 'oo' sound – for which instead we have 'yeessless' (useless), 'fieeneral' (funeral), 'nyeespaper' (newspaper), and in a shop the other day I found a *printed* package advertising the contents as 'A Space Saving Sollition'.

Does this matter? Well, the 'oo' sound does, for actors and singers. It's a sound that very often needs to be *sustained* in speech, particularly at the ends of lines in verse. In Act V Scene 2 of *Love's Labour's Lost* we have this exchange:

ROSALINE: My face is but a moon, and clouded too.
KING: Blessed are clouds, to do as such clouds do.

Shakespeare has chosen the words 'moon', 'too' and 'do' because their sound will carry to the back of the theatre. The pinched 'ee' sound, by contrast, is impossible to sustain with any power. Singers know that. 'Somewhere there's myeesic – how high the meeun . . . ' just doesn't work.

Apart from all that, why is R.P. (if it still exists in its natural form) of any use to us as actors? Well, simply that certain texts, in order to work, need to be spoken in the way the playwright heard them in his mind when writing the words. Shaw, Coward, Wilde all need that particular diction, otherwise they sound artificial, *wrong*. The same goes for television adaptations of Victorian novels; you have to adopt a style of speech that convinces the audience that you're happy with the language.

I have a slightly ambivalent attitude towards the term R.P.; I believe there could and should be a sort of Actor's English – clear, resonant, and adaptable for all non-dialect parts. After all, singers in English have to manage it, getting the full resonance on 'ah', 'ay' and 'oo' sounds – actors should achieve it too, without sounding affected or over-privileged.

Sometimes when either of us is teaching or directing we come across a sort of inverted snobbery about this dreadful term. An actor will often diligently study the accent of a Newcastle shipbuilder, a Devonshire farmer or a Birmingham businessman, but will jib at learning from recorded examples of R.P., feeling that his or her own natural speech is somehow being disparaged. I tell them, how you speak normally is no concern of mine or anyone else's, but why can't you learn

R.P. as just another dialect? It'll be useful, I promise.

I feel passionately about dialect and different accents – not simply foreign or regional dialect, but the infinite variety of 'class' accents in Britain.

For years now I have been trying to publish a CD of various 'posh' English accents, with the aid of the brilliant speech expert, Patsy Rodenburg. We spent many fascinating hours at the British Library listening to different recorded manifestations of posh English: Army-speak, Navy-speak, RAF-speak (quite loud), aristocratic speech of various periods, diplomatic, clerical and legal speech, academic speech, and so on – all subtly but noticeably different. Alas, we were unable to get the funding to produce the record, but I hope one day it may be possible. Meanwhile, when playing a character with a noticeable accent, try to obtain an appropriately accurate recording of that accent early on in rehearsal, or even beforehand if the director agrees and is in sympathy.

ORCHESTRAL DEMANDS OF TEXT

This may be more a subject for directors, but particularly with plays, and indeed all texts written before 1910 – when there wasn't universal literacy, so everything was designed to be read aloud – the sound of the words is an essential element of the writing.

When you're rehearsing in a small room, playing a love-scene or a ferocious argument with someone three feet away in jeans and a T-shirt, the heightened language of Shakespeare can at first seem inflated, embarrassing and plainly silly. So I think you should take your partner into a big space somewhere, and have a shout – discover what is needful, vocally and physically to *realise* the text – find what, for example, Shakespeare was hearing in his mind's ear when he wrote, 'Blow, winds, and crack your cheeks . . . ', and also to justify the poesy and rhetoric of the language you're using. Then during rehearsal, try to substantiate that power and volume in psychological terms – rather as opera singers have to – without resorting to untruthful over-the-top acting. It's something which directors and actors sometimes fail to consider, as fashion appears to demand smaller, intimate performing spaces providing audiences with a more televisual experience.

PHRASING

Acquire good phrasing – for one thing, it will help you to useful work in voice-overs. Phrasing is a subject often ignored in modern training. The principle of single stress – that is, one main stress in each grammatical sentence – is generally not taught in Drama Schools, and often not understood by today's actors, or indeed teachers, possibly owing to the decline in or absence of grammar instruction in modern education. When I say to a drama class, 'Don't stress prepositions and particles unless you're meant to be a politician or a presenter of the weather forecast: when in doubt go for the *noun*', they say, 'What's a preposition?' So the explanation might take two minutes – examples are, 'I have been working *IN* my constituency *ON* the question *OF* crime prevention *FOR* the benefit *OF* the local residents. . . .'

Following the explanation, doors seem to open for most of the class, and they come up to me in the coffee break saying, 'Why didn't we learn this at Drama School?' Below is a list of the 'Principles of Stress' that I've collated over the years, and which young actors seem to find useful. Our son Samuel West is an actor and director, and gives occasional workshops, at the end of which he distributes these notes, entitling them 'Ma's Principles of Stress, or If You Can Phrase Properly You Will Earn More Money'.

SOME PRINCIPLES OF STRESS IN SPOKEN ENGLISH

Observe these principles for the sake of (a) clarity, (b) variety and (c) speed.

Ignore them, sometimes, for the sake of (a) sense and (b) character.

1 Assume that there is only *one* main stress in every grammatical sentence.

2 Stress nouns before adjectives, and verbs before adverbs. When in doubt, go for the *noun.*

3 Don't colour 'colour words': e.g. 'vibrant', 'brilliant', 'rolling', 'pomp',

'terror' etc – they have been deliberately chosen to work for themselves.

4 Don't stress negatives – they should also work for themselves.

(To Frank Hauser, a director very demanding about the delivery of text, this was a particular bugbear. An actor in rehearsal might declare, 'I have *NO* spur to prick the sides of my intent', and a shout would come from the back of the stalls: 'Nobody said you had!' To Portia's observation that 'the quality of mercy is *NOT* strained', Frank would retort: 'Whoever thought it *was*?')

5 Don't stress personal pronouns and possessive adjectives (I, me, my, mine, you, your, his, her, etc). They are strong enough and don't usually need help.

6 Let subordinate clauses ride without stress or emphasis; also phrases in brackets or any form of parenthesis. Also look at the possibility of saying them all on one note. This will allow you to take them as slowly or as quickly as you like.

7 Don't stress prepositions, conjunctions or particles unless playing newsreaders, sports reporters or any other users of 'Media-speak'.

8 In compound verbs, go for the *main* verb, not the auxiliary e.g. don't say 'Much HAVE I travelled in the realms of gold' or 'I WILL arise and go now.' (except when arguing, or playing users of 'Media-speak').

9 Don't make heavy weather of titles, formal phrases of introduction, vocative phrases such as 'Good my Lord', 'Nay, I protest Madam', etc., or casual oaths such as 'Odds my life', 'Pox on't', 'For Christ's sake', etc; often they are there only as courtesies, rhythmic aids or to draw attention to the speaker. In Restoration Comedy particularly, it is often useful to take whole phrases on the 'upbeat', like anacrusis in music, i.e. unstressed notes before the first bar-line.

SOME EXTRA POINTS IN THE SPEAKING OF VERSE

1 Observe contractions: 'Smil'st', 'cunning'st', 'splitt'st', etc. The poet intends the unusual sound, and it is wrong to correct or re-expand it to 'smilest', 'cunningest', 'splittest', etc.

2 Look out for similar-sounding adjacent consonants, 'led to', 'like

cousins', 'and down', etc; often to mark them separately will sound affected or academic, but sometimes the poet may intend the distinction to be made.

3 Don't be afraid to breathe at commas, as well as at full stops.

4 Look out for lines of monosyllables; e.g. 'and slew him thus', 'Why, we have galls; and though we have some grace', 'I do not know why yet I live to say this thing's to do'. *Sometimes* it can indicate that each word should be stressed, or given a specially measured delivery.
5 Don't insert 'ah's and 'oh's, or sighs or gasps into the text; poets usually provide any they want and to add extra ones can spoil the rhythm.

6 Enjambment means when a line of verse 'runs on' to the next. Before an enjambment, breathe well at the beginning of the sentence, then take it steadily, not rushing round the corner, letting the word at the end of the line have its due weight, but *not* 'lifting' it to indicate the enjambment. Example:

SONNET XXIX
'...And then my state
(Like to the lark at break of day arising
From sullen earth) sings hymns at
heaven's gate.'

It also helps to hit the first words of the second line quite hard.

Two sophisticated points:

Lists: When you have 'lists' of words or phrases, separated by commas, be aware that to lift the inflection on each creates an expectation of further words or phrases in the list, i.e. it will sound literary and prepared. If you want to sound spontaneous, as though the character is thinking up each addition as he speaks, repeat the inflection you would use on the first word if it stood alone.

Antithesis: In general, don't anticipate the second statement, it is more elegant to deliver the first statement as if it were going to stand alone, then pick out the sense of the second: e.g. 'From me far off, with others all too near.' Or: 'Ninety-nine per cent of the people in the world are fools; and the rest of us are in great danger of contagion.' *Don't* lift the inflection on 'fools' at the end of the first statement, thus anticipating the joke. Again,'Marriage is a bribe to make a housekeeper think she's a house*holder*' – not 'Marriage is a bribe to make a house*keeper* think she's a house*holder*.'

One further point about phrasing. I've noticed that people who read music, or at any rate know how to do so, have an instinctive idea about phrasing; and I think this must be because they subconsciously picture the line of text on a musical stave – with bar-lines, time-signatures and dynamics. A lot of dramatists (Oscar Wilde, Noël Coward, Harold Pinter, David Mamet, Joe Orton spring immediately to mind) seem to write almost according to musical notation. You have to get the phrasing right, or you won't, in crude terms, get the laugh, or the shiver.

SOLILOQUY

'Who am I supposed to be talking to when I'm alone on the stage?' It's a perfectly proper question to ask. Modern writers of course use the convention in a variety of ways, but in classical drama soliloquies fall into three distinct categories, depending on the direction in which they are aimed: let's call them Outward, Upward or Inward. The *Outward* approach is the obvious one, directed at the audience who are there that night: the Chorus in *Henry V*, Shakespeare's clowns and his cynical commentators like Thersites and Autolycus; Iago of course uses the device all the time, taking the audience into his confidence, and indeed so does the playwright himself in the person of Prospero at the end of *The Tempest*: 'Now my charms are all o'erthrown . . . '

The *Upward* address is the character's appeal to a higher authority: God, Nature, Fate, whatever. It could be a demand for divine justification, compassion or support: Macbeth's 'Come, seeling night', Juliet's 'Gallop apace, you fiery-footed steeds', Othello's 'It is the cause', or Lear's call for sympathetic elemental activity: 'Blow winds, and crack your cheeks . . . '

The *Inward* address means, literally, talking to oneself; weighing arguments aloud, trying out ideas in the privacy of one's own brain: Hamlet's 'To be, or not to be', Henry V's 'Upon the king!', Leontes' 'Too hot! Too hot!'

One might imagine a general guide for the delivery of these three kinds of soliloquy: a fairly robust approach for the Outward, a heightened, rhetorical style for the Upward, while a more introspective, contemplative manner would be more appropriate for the Inward. In fact, though, a survey of some of the better-known speeches in this last category reveals switch-back vertiginous flights of inner turmoil, demanding considerable intellectual agility from the actor.

LEARNING THE LINES

The question most often asked of actors by members of the public is, 'How ever do you learn all those words?' The answer changes over the years, and depends on the nature of the work. In rep it was a discipline – forget the truth or the subtext, get the lines learnt by Wednesday, and worry about the rest of it later if you have the time. But even in ideal circumstances, where early rehearsals are spent discussing the text, improvising scenes, building the inner life of characters and so on, it's essential to get on top of the lines as soon as you can.

I always used to be nervous about learning lines before the very start of rehearsals, for fear of getting set ideas about the part and being found inflexible to work with, but I now think that's wrong: it doesn't make you set in your ways, on the contrary the confidence that comes from knowing the lines makes you more adaptable.

I disagree. The play on the page is one thing; once the words begin to be spoken aloud by other people, it becomes something quite other. However, of course much of the work of learning the lines has to be done privately. Some people have a fixed procedure – mnemonics, going down the page with a postcard, writing them out in longhand, recording them and then playing them back; while others, myself for instance, can only do it by simply reading the play over and over again. Some scripts are much easier to learn than others, and this has a lot to do with the quality of the writing; strong images, natural expression, well-structured arguments tend to impress themselves accurately on the memory, while on the other hand, careless writing – which you think you could have put better yourself – on the whole doesn't.

It is, I think, unreasonable to expect total word-for-word accuracy from a cast by the end of the second week of rehearsal; but it can be maddening for the director and your fellow actors if someone keeps stopping and asking for a prompt. My own way of coping with this is temporarily to paraphrase – conveying the meaning and eliciting the right response, without allowing the scene to lose momentum. After the rehearsal, whoever is 'on the book' can point out the areas where your invention has been particularly wild, and you can pay special attention to revising those sections when you get home.

Having said all this, it is of course the actor's final responsibility to deliver the lines exactly in the form in which they were written. The playwright, we must suppose, has chosen those words, and arranged them in that way, for a good reason, and probably after much thought. To be inaccurate in their delivery, either carelessly or deliberately, is disrespectful and dishonest.

'I WOULD NEVER SAY THAT . . . '

Regrettably, we do encounter young actors who from time to time in rehearsal dig their toes in and maintain that their character couldn't possibly say, do or think what the text has laid down for them. Confusing your own personality and psychological make-up with that of the character is obviously a bad mistake, but so is an inability to take into account the social mores of different places and periods. Something

that feels difficult to stomach now may
have been perfectly all right in sixteenth-
century Verona, eighteenth-century Bath
or twentieth-century Mayfair.

SKILLS

Keep up with some of the things you
learned at Drama School – fencing,
dancing, singing particularly. Remember
how to fall over in different ways without
hurting yourself (that always impresses
people). Learn to ride, if you can afford
the lessons, and it's a good thing if you
can swim.

If you're an Equity member, you can go to
classes at the Actors Centre in central
London; there are offices in Coventry,
Sheffffield, Manchester, Glasgow and
Cardiff with a head office in London.

Some parts you play will involve using
tools or equipment with which your
character must seem thoroughly
familiar. Find out as early as you can
about what you may be required to do,
and how it should be done, and get
used to handling the relevant props.
If they're unavailable, practise with a
substitute.

Remember that 'work plays', plays that are set for instance in a kitchen, a workshop, a pear-orchard, are very popular with audiences, who want to see actors doing something other than acting – carving a statue, breaking in a horse, serving High Mass – and doing it convincingly.

LEARNING FROM OTHER PERFORMANCES

A delicate subject; one shouldn't pinch other people's ideas, but it's true that another actor's work can, as it were, open doors and stimulate memories and characterisations of one's own.

I am not squeamish about this: particularly with classical plays, we're all trying to build up the world's sum total of knowledge or understanding about a particular character or situation. Borrowing in these circumstances is no plagiarism: it won't come out the same, because you're you and they're them.

I do believe passionately in an actor's duty to watch other work in all media. It can teach one good habits, and help to overcome bad ones.

REHEARSALS

Nowadays, rehearsal for filming – whether for TV or the cinema – is normally restricted to agreeing the text, exploring the set and running through the scene a couple of times. For a full-length play in the live theatre, however, four weeks is the normal allotment of time before the first preview, though the subsidised national companies may allow six or even eight weeks.

Arrive punctually on the first day (and indeed at all times thereafter: this is very important). You will find yourself in a room full of people, few if any of whom you may have met before, and whose functions you can't altogether determine. The Company Manager will, or should, introduce you to the Creative Team as it is called, and to the stage management, your fellow actors and various other people, and you will for a while make a valiant attempt to remember all their names, and then give up.

On the table will be a model of the set – probably covered over until the moment when the designer wishes to talk about it – and perhaps pinned to the wall a few drawings of the costume designs, which may delight you, or come as a bit of a surprise.

Having had coffee, everyone will sit down round a table or in a semi-circle, and you will read the play through, perhaps after the director has given an introductory talk.

People handle read-throughs in different ways. Some try to give the director an idea of how they propose to do it in performance, others are deliberately non-committal, while others again appear to have difficulty simply in reading aloud. When it's your turn, just do it intelligently, without showing off.

The whole of the first week may be spent in discussing the feeling and language of the play, the background to the story, the characters' motivation and journey throughout the piece, before getting onto your feet. Having an early grip on your lines will be immensely helpful when you start to move around; being able to look a fellow actor in the eyes will dictate to a great extent when you feel the need to move and when not to – impossible if you're still clutching a script.

Sometimes, about halfway through the rehearsal period, a director will feel that, while a lot of attention is being paid to solving individual moments in the play, this is happening at the expense of a through-line, an energy, an overall dynamic.

He or she may suggest an early run-through at performance pitch. This may frighten people – 'We're not ready', they will cry. Go for it. Such conditions require full commitment, no hedging, no com-promises. Jump in at the deep end – then if it works in a general way you can do the fine tuning later. If it doesn't, you'll have a fair idea why, and still have time to do something about it.

One must be *adaptable* to the play, to the writer, the director and one's fellow actors. Be prepared for all approaches, from 'Method' technique to conventional 'blocking'. I believe ultimately that the writing is paramount: one's artistic and moral duty is to deliver the author's work to that night's audience, in the most truthful, persuasive and entertaining way.

SMALL PARTS

'There are no small parts, just small actors.' Easy to say, but undoubtedly some parts *are* smaller than others, have less to do or say, and don't bear the weight of extensive psychological analysis. The messenger is there essentially to deliver a message, the waitress to wait, the stretcher-bearer to bear the stretcher, the liftman to operate the lift. If the author has given you no further information to pass on to the audience, and the director hasn't decided to invest your brief appearance with some unexpected significance, then I'm afraid that's it. You should of course observe and study waitresses, liftmen and the rest, just as carefully as you would if they were the protagonists of the piece, and you must then convince the audience that this is the job you do. You're not an actor pretending to be a milkman while hoping something better will come along; you're a milkman.

Many times I've been struck – particularly in the cinema – by the simple, truthful performance of some non-speaking bystander, and have remembered them afterwards rather more clearly than I did the stars of the picture.

BIG PARTS

The actor playing a 'big' part has a musical responsibility to the author and the audience as well as a psychological, interpretative one. Broadly speaking, it's the same sort of responsibility to the composer and his listeners that the soloist has in a concerto. He must explore the piece for opportunities to develop the shape and the dynamic of his own performance, and justify them in psychological terms.

I think it's helpful to stick with that musical analogy when approaching, say, a Shakespearean tragedy. Sections of the score seem as if they might be marked 'Allegro cantabile', 'Andante', 'Scherzo', 'Allegro furioso' and so on; and to think of them in this way will help you to plan where, for instance, extremes of energy and vocal power are called for to serve the overall dynamic shape, and again, where the audience need to pause for breath.

COSTUME

When rehearsing a period play, it's useful to wear practice garments that approximate to what you'll be wearing in performance. This has the obvious advantage of getting you used to where pockets, if any, will be, how you will need to adjust your coat, dress or skirt when sitting, and for men, the height and stiffness of collars. Essentially, the right clothes (and the right shoes) will help you to achieve the correct stance and deportment for the period

Take care of your stage costumes. My first considerable part when an Acting ASM at the Bristol Old Vic was as the juvenile in Molière's *Le Bourgeois Gentilhomme*, wearing a beautiful period costume. Coming down the stairs from my second-floor dressing room, feeling glamorously in period, I heard a scream from the Wardrobe Mistress: 'Lift your skirt up when you're going downstairs: don't trail your train on the floor until you're on stage.'

Hang everything up when you've taken it off, don't just leave it bunched up on a chair, or on the floor. Powder your neck with talcum when wearing white collars.

Don't eat or drink while you're in costume, or if you must then cover yourself with a towel. It's *your* costume, part of *your* character, and it's your business to look after it.

RESEARCH

I believe passionately in the value of research, provided it doesn't, as it were, show from out front. Eighty per cent of any research you do will quite possibly turn out to be irrelevant, because the factual and historic truth of a situation may well not accord with the playwright's chosen view – but the twenty per cent you're left with can provide you with an invaluable sense of authority.

For instance, in reading the genuine lives of some of Shakespeare's historical characters – Bolingbroke in *Richard II* springs to mind, and indeed Henry V – you'll come up with some very uncomfortable incongruities, but at the same time absorb a lot of useful background.

I've played more than my fair share of 'real' people – people who have actually existed in the past – and of course, in deserving dramatisation they tend to have been generally pretty well documented. Anything you can read by or about such people is well worth while; paintings or photographs, film footage or voice recordings are tremendously helpful, and so are personal reminiscences (though these can be prejudiced and unreliable). Any physical peculiarities should be studied carefully – to take an obvious example, when I played Josef Stalin, learning exactly how he coped with his withered left arm was essential before we even started rehearsal. (Though I have to admit, in 'taking my character home with me' as the journalists like to say, I did overstep the mark in trying for ages to uncork a bottle of wine with one hand.)

It's an actor's artistic duty to study human behaviour of all kinds, and also that of animals. Visits to the zoo, as well as the observation of domestic animals, provide a rich field of behavioural ideas. The habit of observation can become a skill that operates independently of social activity, storing up information for possible future use.

Certain parts may require very specialised study involving more than

ordinary expense of time and money.
(Visits to unfamiliar geographical areas,
for instance, in order thoroughly to
familiarise yourself with local dialect
and custom.) Sometimes – not often –
the management you're working for will
be prepared to finance this, but in any
case remember that any such expen-
diture can be claimed against tax.

DIRECTORS

Directors come from all quarters: there
are writers who want to interpret their
own work, academics who want to lift the
play from page to stage, there are actors-
turned-directors, teachers-turned-
directors, training-school graduates, and,
of course, natural directors.

In the course of their professional lives,
actors may come in contact with several
hundred different directors, few of
whom, however, will have seen any of
their own fellows at work. So they tend to
do things in their chosen way, whilst the
actor gets used to adapting to the
different methods of one director after
another.

I worked once with an American director
who, although he was very brilliant and

ultimately achieved an excellent production, used a vocabulary in rehearsal that struck some of us as pretentious, baffling and impractical. Such instructions as 'You two should have a focus on that line', we would learn to translate as meaning that we might at that point exchange a glance. 'We need to create a physical re-orientation,' he would decide, which provoked a terse response, 'You mean you want me to *move*?' We erected reactionary barriers because as actors we are wary of any sort of directorial approach that seems to threaten our fragile security. Improvisation, role-swapping and games of various kinds all have occasional use in rehearsal, but an intelligent director will be reluctant to introduce such devices until he or she has earned the full confidence of the cast.

Equally of course, it's up to the actors to be generous and not to withhold that confidence. Directors can be just as thin-skinned as actors, we can all benefit by learning new methods, and the essential thing is to feel that everybody is working towards the same end. The director's task is to recognise and to synthesise the various qualities and energies offered by each member of the cast, and to do so in a spirit of harmony.

People sometimes ask, 'What happens if you find you're in serious disagreement with a director?' In my experience, it's hardly ever happened. The autocratic days of Erich von Stroheim and Basil Dean are long gone, but you may occasionally come across someone who believes that their own directorial imprint on the play is far more important than the play itself. If you know you're going to be fundamentally in opposition to a director's attitude even before you start, then you shouldn't do the play. Otherwise, try hard to make things work for you the director's way before confessing that you're defeated.

I need to be *looked after* in rehearsal; encouraged, challenged, pushed; and essentially to be made to feel that I can play the part. I don't care how rigorous or unconventional the method of rehearsal; as long as I remain convinced of the director's belief in me, I'm happy.

WORKING WITH PEOPLE YOU DON'T GET ON WITH

This has been mercifully rare in my working life (at least, as far as I've been made aware), but of course there are times in every actor's life when colleagues seem obstructive, cantankerous and, one feels, possibly miscast.

It's inevitable that a group of actors with their own characters' separate agendas will occasionally express conflicting views; but it's hardly ever worth having a showdown during rehearsals and upsetting fellow actors or the director – so much will develop inwardly, naturally, during the work. Of course it's sometimes very helpful to talk to colleagues, or ask their advice, about scenes which don't quite seem to be working; if so, do it tactfully – in our family it's called, 'Darling, you know the bit where . . . ?'

If there are disagreements, it's in everyone's interests to try and fit in with your colleagues' alternative ideas with as good a temper as possible, until they are patently shown to be wrong.

They may, of course, turn out to be right.

AUDIENCES

Audiences can teach you so much.
Sometimes, their reaction to a text will
help you play it better. Particularly so
with comedy; you may find that for some
reason you don't quite understand, a
particular line will get a much bigger
laugh if you play it in a different way or
from a slightly altered position.
Something you thought would get a
sure-fire reaction surprisingly doesn't,
until you realise that the fault lies in the
delivery of an earlier 'plant' setting up
the joke: it's not been clear enough,
perhaps there was too much going on at
the time, and the focus was blurred.

Fidgets, coughs, sweet-eating, and
nowadays the obsessive recourse to
plastic bottles of water, give their own
clear message.

So do snores.

Mobile phones and chiming watches we
just have to put up with, I suppose.
But audiences do send subtler signals:
their *silences*. When you've been at it
a little while you'll be able to interpret
various different kinds of silence.
There's the delicious pin-drop hush that

tells you they're on the edge of their seats, hanging on your next syllable; and the very different pall of quiet that descends on the house when they're bored, just before the coughing starts. There are two other interesting forms of silence that you can eventually learn to identify: one, signifying that the audience has not quite understood or believed what has just happened, and are waiting to have it made clear; and the other, subtly different, which indicates that although they've enjoyed the play up to now, suddenly they've all concluded that it isn't quite as good as they thought.

Nobody's yet managed to explain why, when confronted with the selfsame production, two audiences of mixed ages, apparently drawn from the same ranks of society, should behave in totally different ways on different nights. There may be one or two individuals among them given to extreme reaction (or non-reaction), but how can they affect the whole *body* of the audience?

You must never let the audience *drive* the show; however much they're lapping it up, you've got to be in control. There are ways in which you can 'play' a comedy audience for instance, like an angler with a fish.

Control their reactions – they might be bursting to laugh at a funny situation, but you are aware, while they aren't yet, that there's a much funnier one coming up in thirty seconds; and if you curtail their laughter on the first gag, they'll enjoy the second far more. It's good to keep the comedic structure of the whole play in mind, and make sure the audience don't tire themselves out too early. Above all, when performing the kind of play in which the wit, the argument, the language has to scintillate, and you feel the audience is having to struggle to keep up, *don't slow down* for them. If you do, their reactions will slow down too, and a pattern of reciprocal deceleration will settle like a shroud. Just keep a carrot's length ahead of them – audiences love working to catch up, we know that ourselves; it's a hugely invigorating sensation.

Some actors, if they're lucky enough to be in a long run, find themselves losing concentration, 'walking through' their parts and finding it difficult to make themselves believe that everything that is happening to them on the stage that night is happening for *the first time.* It sounds easy, teaching yourself to greet each line and situation as being freshly-minted, but in fact in emptying your mind of the future, there's a real danger of emptying it of everything else.

You may find yourself playing to audiences who are unsympathetic to what the writer is saying, but it is our professional job to hold their attention, not by flashy and selfish acting, but by focus on the main line of a scene, and attention to clarity and audibility as well as truth.

Acting, maintained Sir Ralph Richardson, is simply the art of stopping people from getting bored. There are no bad audiences, someone else said: it is your business to create good ones.

I believe passionately in staying flexible throughout the run of a play; though it's as well to consult the feelings of colleagues about potential changes and developments.

I'm not quite sure what Pru means by 'flexible' in this context. The trouble with long runs in the West End is that as your audience of theatrical devotees gives way, after three or four weeks, to more casual playgoers, and later to the tourists from overseas (without whom there would *be* no West End), their reaction to the play must change significantly. Do you try and adapt your delivery to the shifting audience, or remain faithful to the production you rehearsed and opened with?

THE DIFFERENT MEDIA

We've been talking mainly in terms of the demands of live theatre, although delivery of the lines is of course central to the job in all its forms. But let us now look at some of the special consider-ations demanded by film, television and radio.

THE CAMERA

Work in front of the camera, particularly the television camera, is now the central concern of most performers in this country. Much, a great deal too much, is made of the different abilities and qualities expected of the screen actor as opposed to the stage actor, but really common sense dictates an attitude, an appreciation of scale, a paring down to essentials, that is required for the vernacular, super-naturalistic world of most TV drama.

Experience in camera technique and the chance to see your work played back on screen should have been an essential part of your training. In the Old Days – for want of a better expression – you didn't get to see 'rushes' unless you were a big star, so only at the premiere could you notice your own bad habits – grimacing, blinking, finger-wagging, etc – and groan with frustration and shame.

These days, there's almost always a monitor on the set, where the director can show you an instant replay of any scene, and sometimes be persuaded to shoot it again if you're really unhappy with what you see. But in any case, you should have had ample opportunities during your training to correct bad habits and develop good ones.

When acting for the camera the essential thing to understand is that nothing needs to be signalled or indicated: think the right thoughts, and your eyes will tell the story. Leave the rest of your face alone.

Eyes are the windows of the soul, the great arbiter of sincerity. It used to be remarked that the witch-hunting Senator Joseph McCarthy, of the House Un-American Activities Committee, was able to convince a room full of people of his sincerity when he propounded his appalling doctrine, but that the first TV close-up revealed the dangerous mania behind those eyes.

As in the theatre, make sure we see those eyes – i.e. don't look down too much or too often; when speaking to another character, look at *one* of their eyes – the downstage one, or on screen the one nearest the camera. And try not to blink.

Try to understand what the camera can do, and what it can't. Learn about lenses. Find out from the camera operator what lens is being used for each shot, and consequently the size in which your face or body will appear. Ask yourself whether what you are doing may seem not clear enough in one shot, or too pronounced in another. When you're being filmed in close-up, your colleague with whom you're playing the scene will be positioned next to the camera, giving you their 'off-lines' and enabling you to play to them. When the situation is reversed, tuck yourself in as near the lens as you can, in order to give your partner a good eye-line to the camera, which is representing your own face.

WORKING IN FILMS

Probably the most difficult exercise for an actor moving for the first time from stage to screen is simply adjusting to the working environment. In the theatre, apart from the half-acknowledged presence of the audience, your visible world is peopled simply by those actors involved in the scene with you. When filming however, your concentration has to be maintained in the face of a whole crowd of technicians, lights trained on you from unexpected angles, perhaps a focus-puller or a boom operator lying full-length just in front of you.

Instead of going through a linear recital of your character's story, as you do in the theatre, here you'll be examining a tiny episode out of context, trying to think what sort of a person you are at that particular point in the story, and having to repeat the perhaps 45-second section over and over again, from different angles and on different lenses.

Beavering away in intense detail at that one tiny scene until you've got it as right as you can, then clearing your mind ready for the next bit (which will almost certainly not be in story sequence) is a discipline entirely different from that required for the live theatre, but believe me, it does bring its own peculiar satisfaction.

A word about the broad differences between the cinema and TV industries in this country. English-speaking film production can now be regarded as falling roughly into two distinct categories. Firstly, there are films dealing with stories on a human scale – comedies, thrillers, romantic subjects. They cost anything up to about $100 million to make, and have a reasonable expectation of recoupment in cinemas round the UK, on the east and west coasts of the United States, in Australia, New Zealand and a few other areas. Such pictures, though made in this country, will probably demand an American star or two in order to achieve effective distribution, but at the same time will provide opportunities for British supporting actors who can deliver the goods.

The second category is the Blockbuster: expensive, special-effects-driven, action movies that will need to be seen world-wide to recover their costs – in other words, to be distributed in non-English-speaking countries where they don't like dubbing or subtitles, and for whom dialogue therefore has to be kept to a minimum. They obviously offer fewer opportunities to actors, but you could be fortunate, and if you are, you will make a *lot* of money.

To put your initial energy into getting into the world of films would be a mistake. Film work is very intensive, and those involved in it are often isolated from what is going on in television and the theatre. If you're dying to work in the movies, you really have to forget about doing anything else. Pawn your body and soul, Faustus-like, to the exigencies of the movie industry, because you will need to be constantly available to meet directors in mad places at no notice and, once you're actually filming, to fit in with rewrites, rescheduling, overrunning, delays due to weather, strikes, re-shoots or the failure of the investors to come up with the ready. You will have to be prepared, with bags packed, to fly to Montevideo at 7.00 tomorrow morning, only to be told just as you go to bed that you won't be needed for another fortnight. Then next morning they'll ring you again to bring your flight forward to Wednesday, and it won't be Montevideo, it'll be Riyadh, and of course you can ride a camel?

This sort of thing can be very exciting: it can also be very stressful. Repeating the same fragmentary scene time after time after time because of aeroplane noise, camera wobble, someone – you, maybe – fluffing a line or not quite hitting their marks on the floor, while freezing to death in steady rain as the director fumes about losing the light, can make one think longingly of those polite matinées at the Salisbury Playhouse.

Also, before you commit yourself to seeking a career in films, ask yourself whether your face is really suited to the cinema screen. Be brutally honest and try to imagine how it will look in enormous close-up. The question is not one of beauty, elegance, symmetry, or spectacular ugliness, but whether each individual square centimetre of your face is going to be *interesting* enough when expanded to fill that enormous area. My own face, for instance, doesn't pass the test, harbouring between eyes and mouth an expanse of photographic irrelevance. I'm glad I recognised this early on, and decided my features were more suited to the small screen, or better still, the theatre.

The various processes leading up to a film's final release may occupy a year or more. By the time you get to see a picture you were in, you will probably have forgotten the whole experience of making it. Having worked on the project for perhaps five weeks, you may feel that your appearance in the final print might have been accomplished in five hours. You suddenly remember favourite moments that just aren't there any more. You seem to be in soft focus a great deal, and the editor appears to have been fascinated by the back of your head.

Well, sorry, that's movies for you.

WORKING IN TELEVISION

Television is rather different. Ideally it should represent the effective fusion of film and theatre. When television production in this country re-started after World War II, actors were recruited from the established ranks of the West End theatre. The BBC studios were in

London, so why look further? Film people (we had a very successful film industry in the 1950s) didn't want to know, anyway.

It didn't take long for the actors to acquire the basic disciplines required – many of them had some experience of camera work for the cinema – and a few of those early efforts would probably stand black-and-white comparison with some of what we see today, though some would strike us now as stagey and over-explanatory compared with the naturalism of today's regular series. In those formative days of both BBC and ITV Drama, the star attraction each week was the regular Single Play, pieces written by top TV dramatists expressly for the medium, which each week introduced the audience to different characters in a fresh environment and unrelated situations. Gradually though, the focus turned towards genre drama, series centred round a regular group of characters in a particular set of circumstances, and while in some ways this provided actors with rather less in the way of artistic range, it meant, for the first time, regular work and a chance to continue to play a single character over a period of months, or even years.

Only in the last couple of decades has TV drama moved away from being performed in one continuous session, in the studio, with the shots offered by four or more different video-cameras being selected up in the control room by the video mixer, instructed by the director and laid down in a 'camera script' which will have been prepared during the week or two's preliminary rehearsal in a church hall somewhere. Now most television is shot on location; in many ways like a cinema film, though using lighter equipment and fewer staff, dispensing almost entirely with rehearsal, and covering a great deal of ground in the course of a working day.

Some comedy series (not all) are still performed in the studio, with multiple cameras and a live audience. Some actors (me included, but not Pru, she likes it) find problems with performing to two different audiences simultaneously: two hundred people on a grandstand, a couple of viewers on a sofa. You mustn't of course *play to* the studio audience, who aren't supposed to be there, but you have to accommodate their reactions and laughter, just as you would in the theatre.

Television comedy should – indeed must – depend as much on credibility of situation and character as does any detective or hospital series. People often ask: who was Sibyl Fawlty based on? The answer is, on no particular person, but on a number of different characteristics and mannerisms that the writing suggested from my memory. Sibyl's background, her early relationship with Basil, and the conditions which led them to marry, deserve as much consideration as would Mrs Alving's circumstances, Madame Arkadina's or Lady Bracknell's.

I can't remember who it was that said films make you rich, television makes you famous, but the theatre is what it's all about. Certainly, if you're playing a significant part in a popular series, television can turn you overnight into a household name. Such visibility also can put you near the top of the list when a play is being cast on tour or for the West End. It is important, though, not to overdo your TV service as PC Smith, Staff Nurse Jones or Leading Fireman Robinson. You may find, when you finally move on, that people are now unwilling to accept you as anything else.

I believe the whole phenomenon and culture of television can, or should, give a huge boost to the acting profession. Unfortunately, there is a tendency among casting directors to categorise actors – oh, yes, you're a theatre actor aren't you – oh no, he does more the comedy shows . . . A good actor should be proficient in all media. If you've been working in the theatre and haven't quite made it into television, write to some producers and directors whose work you've seen and try to get them to give you a camera test or at least an interview. The medium can always use new talent, and many Series Producers are particularly concerned to find untried, unfamiliar faces.

Signing up for crowd work through a crowd artists' agency, and keeping your eyes and ears open, is another possible way in.

WORKING IN RADIO

In many ways my favourite medium – there are fewer character restrictions, and the scenery is so much more lavish . . . Not very tall myself, I once played the immensely-long-legged revue artist Mistinguette in a radio play; and on my fiftieth birthday, I took the leading part of a seven-year-old child. However, not all actors enjoy radio, they miss being able to use their eyes and bodies.

Worrying about this can lead to *poor* radio acting – trying to suggest to the listener what you would be doing physically if only they could see you. The voice, if you're using it truthfully and not *signalling* with it, will convey everything that needs to be conveyed. And don't be afraid of pausing when it seems right to do so: in life we constantly leave pauses when we're thinking what to say or digesting what someone else has said. So don't worry: they won't switch off.

Nowadays one can rehearse the text alone at home and play it back on tape – useful, I think, though it would probably have been frowned on in the Old Days – 'Don't want to lose your spontaneity, dear.' Rubbish. Artificial spontaneity is part of the job: to be able in any medium to recreate and use something that has occurred spontaneously in rehearsal.

You can write in to the BBC Radio Drama Department (address at the end of this book), asking to join the list for a general audition. Work up a really good audition, short and succinct but demonstrating skilful phrasing, mastery of style, and proficiency in a couple of dialects that you can *really* do.

Don't ever think of Radio as the poor relation. If your audition has been successful, and they offer you a contract with the Radio Drama Company, seize it greedily. It's an opportunity to play a huge number of parts, of many different styles, and the experience will tell you a great deal about writing, technique, sincerity, and about yourself.

COMMERCIALS

Personally, I'm grateful for Commercial work, though there are some actors who don't do it on principle (is this snobbery, or lack of opportunity, or do they have private incomes?). I'd certainly refuse to say anything about a product that I didn't know to be true, and a lot of Commercials, as we know, are quite brilliantly written nowadays. Everyone accepts the cynical reality that we look to well-paid Commercial employment to finance ill-paid work in the subsidised theatre.

It used to be felt that performing in vision in Commercials put you in danger of being associated exclusively and for ever with the product you are advertising, and consequently rendered you useless for anything else. On the whole the public are wiser now, and are aware that the authoritative woman who was trying to sell them a washing powder is just another actress really, yes, we saw her last week in *Midsomer Murders.*

Commercial voice-overs can be a source of reassuringly speedy income, if you can get on the bandwagon. Get a CD made (there are many recording studios offering this service – there is a list in *Contacts*) using your own natural voice together with a range of cartoon and character voices if you're happy with that sort of thing, and give it to your agent, or there is a list in *Contacts* of particular agencies who deal specifically in voice-overs, and you can call in, be charming, and leave them a copy of your CD and personal details.

Extolling the virtues of a particular washing powder, dog food or four-wheel-drive vehicle may not do a great deal for your sense of artistic achievement, but I personally find a certain fascination in exploring different ways to utter your twelve-word message of blandishment, and in taking exactly 4.25 seconds to do it. In a curious way, the experience teaches a new respect for the exactitude of language.

CRITICS

Professional criticism is essential to the practice and development of any art form. Though we may be persuaded to consider drama critics generally as a bunch of carping, opinionated ignoramuses, every so often someone like Kenneth Tynan comes along and puts down new guidelines for the development and standards of theatrical practice.

Usually critics are keen to deny that they have any real influence over theatre attendances. Up to a point, they're right; but where they do undoubtedly wield influence is over a new straight play by an unknown writer. Such plays often attract reviews differing so widely that one is led to question whether the critics were actually watching the same play; but alas, a single damning one- or no-star review in a leading broadsheet can do lasting damage to a production. If we are involved in such a show, we have charitably to remember that the critic is simply expressing his personal opinion, which may not be that of anyone else.

I'm afraid I don't read criticisms of plays I'm in until the production has been running several weeks. Of course, if the notices are so bad that the production comes off sooner than that, it's a different scenario, but there's a danger, if the notices are flattering, of becoming smug; or if they're hostile, of feeling too depressed to go on. There is a real danger in the temptation to alter your performance slightly to cope with particular critical cavils: if you're not careful, this can introduce a virus to threaten the bodily health of the production.

Many shows happily survive bad reviews. Finally we have to have faith in our own judgement, whether or not that judgement runs contrary to that of the pundits. Think of the number of times we visit a show that has been lauded with rapturous notices, and can't for the life of us think why.

All I'm trying to say is, that we should serve the author, the director, the

production and our fellow artistes,
before we try to please the critics.

I used to read my own notices avidly, and
then, I can't remember why – possibly I'd
had a run of bad ones – I stopped buying
them, and, like Pru, only glanced at the
occasional one some while after the
opening night. I now think perhaps I
acted hastily. Critics, on the whole, know
their stuff, and it's a wise actor who can
summon the occasional humility to learn
from what they say.

Antony Sher, in his autobiography *Beside
Myself,* puts it rather well: 'Reviews are
like cigarettes. They can give you a buzz,
they can also make you feel sick. Either
way, they're not good for you, yet they're
addictive. You give them up, you start
again, you stop, you tell yourself just one
won't hurt . . . ' For the traumatised
victim, Alan Bennett has these words of
comfort: 'Critics are like eunuchs – they
watch it being done every night, but they
can't do it themselves.'

III

PERSEVERANCE

THE UNPREDICTABILITY OF THE BUSINESS

Let us suppose you have now settled in, but that after an initial run of good luck, things currently seem to have ground to a shuddering halt.

It's important not to get too depressed by this. Self-doubt is an admirable quality in an actor, but can be carried too far. My father, also an actor, would throughout his whole life interpret any lull in the demand for his services as evidence of a comprehensive and perpetual boycott. 'It's no good, I'm in the gutter,' he would declare mournfully, pouring himself a glass of quite respectable claret.

There is, as I said before, no logic in this business; but if you have acquitted yourself well in what you've done so far, your name will gradually find its way onto the lists of actors that are drawn up, in order of preference, every time a project is being cast. Your getting the part will depend upon those who are above you in the pecking order being busy, unwell, too expensive or moving to California. Or else a maverick casting director determined to buck the trend and go for an original choice. You just have to be patient; but – as I also said before – the more different contacts you have made in your early days, the more lists you will now be on, and the shorter time you should have to wait before something turns up. Try to keep these contacts alive. Just because directors haven't asked you back a second time, it doesn't mean you've been entirely forgotten; it's not a bad idea to jog their memory occasionally. Writing to congratulate them, for instance, on a show of theirs you've just seen and liked gives you the opportunity to remind them of your existence.

In the meantime morale must be boosted, and bills paid.

BEING OUT OF WORK

In the UK at any one time two thirds of the female members of Equity are out of work – a situation everyone in the business has to face, sooner or later (well, nearly everyone). Of course the financial problems will have to be faced first (suggestions later), but the equally severe emotional problems must also be coped with: 'Oh God, I'm no good, nobody likes working with me, was I boring in that last play, do I smell or something?' The out-of-work depression problem can be dealt with in various ways: one, is to go to Class.

THE ACTORS CENTRE

Anyone who is a member of Actors Equity is qualifed to enter for classes at the Actors Centre in Tower Street, near Leicester Square in London. An hour in the coffee bar, where there is a notice board advertising jobs and classes, may well provide you with useful information as well as sympathy, and you can also spend a little while keeping yourself fit for whatever turns up next. It's worth thinking too about preparing some new audition pieces that explore new ground for you, and which – possibly with help from some of the excellent tutors at the Actors Centre – might land you the next job.

WRITING AND DEVISING

Of course, if you have a talent for writing, and can thus fill your periods of unemployment creatively, use it to the full. Some actors, while they have a talent for writing generally, prefer to put their literary efforts into outlets other than drama. Getting a play read and approved for the theatre takes ages, and for television only slightly less so; but sketches for TV comedy or short stories for radio can come to fruition within a reasonable time-span. Anything you write and have accepted for production on the Fringe may also be snapped up quite quickly; it will probably do more for your creative satisfaction than for your pocket, but of course you can present your work as vehicles for your own performance.

Also, as we've already suggested, think about preparing recital programmes, either alone or with one or two colleagues. They're often in demand for various festivals and other occasions, and can be a useful resource both financially and in terms of giving you the chance to show your paces in areas in which casting directors don't necessarily think of you.

Offering your services as a script-reader for a management or a literary agency can earn you a little extra money. You will be given a number of scripts to wade through, usually by unknown authors, and be required to read each one and append fairly detailed comments. It's very hard work. According to your initial valuation, the script will then be passed either to a more senior reader or back to the unfortunate playwright. A list of literary agents can be found in *The Writers' and Artists' Yearbook,* published annually by Bloomsbury Publishing.

TEACHING

As you get older, you may even find you have a certain amount to impart to younger actors in a teaching capacity – and the Actors Centres, for instance, are always open to suggestions for classes. The fees offered are modest, but they are better than nothing, and it's a valuable means of keeping in practice.

As with acting itself, all the best teachers I've ever known have been concerned with the *work,* the subject, not with themselves. This goes for the teachers at my school in Eastbourne, as well as those at the Old Vic. Margaret Blackstock taught us Art – not only painting and drawing, but Art History – leaving us with a feeling for period, style, architecture and costume which was later reinforced at the Old Vic School by Litz Pisk. Heather Bell, who taught History at school, was the first Labour voter I had come across, and gave us an amazing insight into foreign politics. Edith Tizzard's subject was Ancient History, and so impressed upon our minds the details of every item in Tutankhamun's tomb – although she'd never been to Egypt – that, years after her death when I went there myself and visited the famous tomb, I shed retrospective tears for her remarkable teaching.

Drama at Eastbourne was taught by Mona Swann, who had been at the forefront of the Choral Speech movement. Choral Speech was part of the curriculum, and though I suspect our efforts were something of an embarrassment for parents at the showings, they were a brilliant way of exploring various verse forms, and indeed learning by heart vast swathes of classical and modern poetry, which has stood me in good stead ever since.

I think good teaching comes from an itch – not to shine or demonstrate, but to transmit as efficiently as possible something you've found helpful or interesting or inspiring.

You may – especially if you've just been seen in some high-profile capacity – be asked to give a Master Class, perhaps for a drama course or drama society at school or university, or to an independent group of playgoers. For this it is usual to ask a modest fee, and travel and accommodation expenses if applicable.

You can play these events more or less as you like, but personally I hate the term 'Master Class', suggesting as it does that anything the participants show you, you can do better – by no means necessarily true. If I'm invited to do one, I prefer to call it a 'Surgery'; I invite those who are having difficulties with a play, a scene, a speech, to come up and tell me about it; we discuss the symptoms and conduct an examination. I try a diagnosis, and suggest a cure. It seems to work, and is perhaps a more collaborative and democratic exercise than the traditional Master Class. Pru calls hers 'Workshops'.

The growth of educational outreach programmes now operated by most regional and touring companies means that this has become a significant specialist area of employment. English Touring Theatre, for instance, faces such an enormous demand for their outreach services around the country, that they employ four such actor/teachers on a full-time basis. It's hard work, mind you.

TEMPORARY JOBS

Obviously it's an advantage to acquire any skill that can earn you the rent when you're not working. Speaking personally, I'm not computer-literate, and have been extraordinarily lucky anyway in having had fairly regular employment, but there was a time before I was married when I shared a flat with three other girls and suddenly found myself pushed for the rent (which was all of £8 a week in those days). One of my flatmates was working for *Which* magazine and got me a temporary job delivering carefully coded anonymous packs of margarine to consumers all over London, for their comments. These extra-curricular jobs can be useful; also you meet 'real people' rather than other actors, and you can save up your impressions and experiences to feed your professional work. (I'm not suggesting actors aren't real – just that their job is pretending to be other people, so the more you know about the 'other people', the better.)

When I was out of work, I used to do a bit of home-decorating for friends and acquaintances. A relaxing job, particularly if the owner wasn't there; satisfying, finite, and a great opportunity to listen to recordings and broadcasts of plays and stories while wielding the paint brush. Really do learn how to put up wallpaper, though, before you accept such a commission. Having to buy new rolls of hand-printed paper to cover your mistakes will cost you more than your whole fee for the job.

WORK YOU CAN'T AFFORD TO DO

The statistics about unemployment for actors are trotted out with regularity, but what is not so generally understood is that there is at any one time quite a lot of work on offer that people simply cannot afford to do. I'm talking mainly about subsidised small-scale touring. A good deal of important and exciting work is done under these conditions, but many of such Arts Council revenue-funded companies can only afford to pay salaries that are insufficient to support an actor with dependents or a mortgage. Such a contract may be for four weeks' rehearsal, and then eight or ten weeks' touring round the country. During those three months you will therefore be unable to fit in the more lucrative voice-over or day's filming that you'd normally seek to bridge the gap, and you may find, alas, that you'd be better off filling that time driving a mini-cab.

If you can *possibly* make such an engagement work economically – perhaps by sub-letting your flat while you're on tour – do it, both for your own sake and for the sake of those audiences many of whom, without the work of such companies, probably would have no experience at all of the live theatre.

TOURING

The dispiriting scenario I've described above fortunately doesn't typify touring conditions in general. Look upon touring as the arterial supply of theatrical life-blood to the nation, and you will perhaps agree with me that those rigidly metropolitan-based actors who refuse (or whose agents refuse on their behalf) to step beyond the bounds of the M25, are being unreasonable and ungenerous. Why should we expect the critical and enthusiastic audience spread across the UK to come hundreds of miles to see us? We have to go to *them* sometimes.

Overseas touring used to be on a much larger scale than it is today: companies of thirty actors and musicians travelling across Europe, the Middle East, Africa, China and Japan. The fact that this doesn't happen on this scale anymore is explained by the British Council (who frequently arranged and co-financed these tours) being determined to show 'British Culture' as it currently is, rather than digging back through the classical repertoire. So they prefer modern plays with only four or five in the cast. Such a tour can be hard work, but a wonderful experience.

Of course all touring means upheaval, living out of suitcases, finding accommodation, and being temporarily separated from loved ones. An appetite for travel, an interest in unfamiliar places, a wanderlust, are the ideal characteristics for the touring actor.

There are still theatrical 'digs' – not so many as there once were, but since the bulk of large-scale touring involves large casts of singers and dancers, the provision of sufficient affordable accommodation is still essential. In middle-scale venues like Cambridge, Oxford, Bath or Malvern, used as they are to the smaller casts of straight drama, there is smaller choice; but up-to-date lists of approved lodgings are kept by theatres, by Equity, by the Actors' Church Union (a helpful body, you don't have to be a communicating Anglican to join), and in that essential publication *Contacts.* Otherwise it's friends in the area, bed-and-breakfasts or, failing everything and seldom to be recommended in this country, cheap hotels.

Particularly for when you're touring abroad, get some easily identifiable luggage, so that you don't waste further time when you're exhausted after your flight, in picking suitcases from the carousel that you thought were yours, and then hefting them back on again when you discover they aren't.

Personally I'm a home bird, and don't really like opening the front door to put the milk bottles out; nevertheless I believe passionately in the principle and the practice of touring, and the responsibility actors have to do it.

We can learn a great deal from the differing regional audiences, and one very important area in which *they* can learn from *us* is in the work of classical companies like English Touring Theatre, who take syllabus-related plays all over the UK in responsible, full-scale productions.

Often pupils from schools in places where we perform have never actually seen a performance of the Shakespeare play they're studying in class, and have been allowed to believe Elizabethan language to be an inflexible barrier to their comprehension. One night, in Crewe, after a performance of *Henry IV Part 1*, in which our son Samuel was Hal and I was playing Falstaff, two fifteen-year-old boys came up to us in the street and told us, 'Hey, that was terrific!' Good, thanks, we said, glad you liked it. 'Yeah, we really *enjoyed* it,' they said. 'We want to know who did the translation.' Sam went off to congratulate our director on having struck a blow for English education, while I wanted to go and burn their school down.

One of the great privileges of touring is being able to play to audiences who might be witnessing a major play for the first time. The sophisticated London audience, coming out of yet another revival of Shakespeare, or Chekhov, or Sheridan, can be heard comparing performances, direction, décor with those of an earlier production – maybe preferable, maybe not, but in either case what has stayed with them have been different *performance elements* of what they've just seen.

I love it when an audience emerges saying what a wonderful *play*, what a wonderful evening in the theatre.

REGIONAL THEATRE

Everything I've said about the importance of touring applies just as much to regional repertory companies. Many towns and cities in the UK have two distinct theatre undertakings which should complement each other: the Playhouse with its resident organisation and identifiable artistic policy having a continuous relationship with the community, and the larger Theatre Royal down the road playing host to national, sometimes star-led, tours of drama, musicals, opera and ballet.

There are very few repertory companies today that carry on the old pattern of keeping an actor for a group of plays, or a whole season. This is partly because nowadays directors like to cast each play independently, from the general pool, and partly because actors themselves are less willing to spend more than a few weeks at a time out of London.

But is London really where you need to be?

WHERE TO LIVE

As someone who never came to London at all until I was a drama student, I'm probably qualified to advocate the advantages of living there as a professional UK actor. Of course, a great deal of the best and most available stage work will be found out of town, and there is still a certain amount of regionally-based television drama produced, but a London base is undeniably useful professionally as well as being potentially a financial asset. As one of the lucky generation who managed to get a reasonable mortgage on a small freehold property in outer London quite early in my married life – my parents, who had never owned their own house, were appalled: 'All that debt hanging over you?' – I do think it pays dividends for an actor to put any savings into property, however modest.

You can always let it privately when working away from home (be generous but not too generous about rent if you're letting to friends) or, if you're really pushed for cash, sell it – usually, if it's anywhere in London, at a profit.

Try and find somewhere convenient for public transport, not too fashionable, and with congenial neighbours.

PUBLIC TRANSPORT

Tim and I devoutly believe in using public transport most of the time – both for environmental and professional reasons. Yes, it's crowded getting into London at peak hours, but certainly quicker than driving – and no parking problems! For thirty-seven years we have lived only twelve minutes' walk from Clapham Junction station. There are also frequent local buses, so we're luckier than most. When working in a London run, I always use public transport, even to come home after the show at night. A very distinguished politician (Labour, at that) was rather

shocked when I told him this recently –
'Aren't you afraid of being accosted, or
even attacked late at night?' But I have
to say that I've never had the smallest
problem coming home from a theatre
(though I was once waylaid round about
midnight in the leafy suburban street
behind our house).

RELATIONSHIPS

It seems highly impertinent to offer
advice on this subject; but we have to
remember that in our profession we are
constantly called upon to relate to a
fellow human being at a very deep level.
Don't confuse stage relationships with
off-stage working relationships, nor
professional alliances with personal
ones.

Marriage. To have one partner in the
acting profession may be regarded as
a misfortune. To have both looks like
carelessness. Perhaps. I'm glad, though,
that I chose to share my life with
someone in the same business. I don't
know how Pru feels about it.

Being married to somebody in the same
business is extremely difficult. I think,

however, being married to somebody who *wasn't* would be impossible.

Listening to your partner's evening grumbles about an exhausting shoot or a bad rehearsal or an audience that's coughed its way through four acts can be quite wearing, but at least you understand; and next week your positions could be reversed. Which couldn't happen if one of you were an estate agent, or a marine re-insurance broker, or a dentist.

CHILDREN

This is a personal, and probably unusual view: having children was one of the best and most useful things that ever happened to me as an actor. Childbirth *expands* you – and not only physically; there's a huge emotional, imaginative and even intellectual expansion involved as well.

Financially disastrous of course, and nowadays I'm afraid much more so than it was thirty years ago; in those days on a meagre salary one could just about afford a live-in au pair or Mother's Help. It cost all the money we had, but meant that we could both go out to work – we could even take the children and the au pair with us where necessary.

I remember breast-feeding our elder son Sam between the acts of *The Promise* at the Fortune Theatre, and saving up £1,300 to take them and the Mother's Help with us on tour to Australia.

MEDIA ATTENTION

You may sometimes find yourself in a situation, probably not of your own making, where some aspect of your personal life, or that of your partner or a colleague, attracts the attention of the popular press. Being lobbied for comment can be very tiresome, but it's a professional hazard and has to be endured.

Physical assault on importunate journalists and photographers, while understandable, is not really recommended – forbearance, courtesy even, will get you off to a better start. It is usually fairly apparent what questions they will want to ask, so it's as well to prepare answers in advance that will appear honest and spontaneous, and if possible entertaining. Be generous about everyone you mention, give every impression of being willing to assist the interviewer, but don't give away more than you feel you have to. And wear something attractive.

PUBLICITY

If you are in a play or film or TV programme, you will be asked to publicise it through interviews in the press or on radio and television. If the show's very successful, journalists and broadcasters will want to interview you anyway. When talking to them try to remember it's the product you're selling, and not yourself. Avoid the words 'I', 'me', 'my' and 'mine', 'my career', and also expressions such as 'I mean', 'you know', 'sort of' – and repetitive gestures and finger-wagging. Talk about the work, the writer, the director, and your colleagues, not about yourself. The important thing is the promotion of the show, rather than your part in it.

During the rehearsal period you may be called away time and time again for interviews or photo-shoots to help the marketing of the play. This can be quite wearing, and often eats into your time off, but it is important, and must be done for the sake of the show. You will find that the same questions are repeated by most of the interviewers; try if possible to vary your answers, and if they seem to be straying from the point guide them gently back to what they should be talking about: what a wonderful show it is, and how much their readers/ viewers/ listeners are going to enjoy it.

Part of the job is to correct journalists' mistaken impressions about the work, one's colleagues, and indeed oneself. I don't want to suggest that all journalists are given to accidental or deliberate distortion; however, whenever I've been interviewed, I now ask to see my own quotes before they're printed. Naturally the writer won't want to show you the whole interview, but you have a legal right to check everything that appears as having been directly said by you, and it's only right to make sure you're quoted in your own words rather than as interpreted by the popular press.

FAN MAIL

Some actors, while being encouraged by any fan mail they get, don't feel that it necessarily requires acknowledgement. I think this is ungenerous. If someone has been kind enough to put pen to paper to compliment you on your performance, it seems only fair to drop them a few lines of thanks, answer any questions they've put to you, or at least send them the signed photograph they've asked for.

If someone asks me for *more* than one signed photograph ('for my friends'), I'm afraid I don't comply: I send just the one, and dedicate it to the sender, 'Best wishes to Gareth (or whoever)'. There is a flourishing trade in autographed performers' photos, sold for profit, and I don't see why this should be carried on at our expense. The cost of the initial photography, reproduction, stationery and stamps mounts up astonishingly.

Occasionally someone, who clearly has never seen or heard anything you've ever done, will write requesting an autograph, fulsomely congratulating you on your performance in a film in which you never appeared, or in which you had no more than a cough and a spit. Bin the letter. They have to learn.

TIPPING

All tips or presents given in the course of your professional employment are allowable against tax, so don't be mean. Leaving something for the stage-doorkeeper every Saturday night (say £5 to £10 when on tour, £10 to £20 in the commercial West End) is not only just, but a sensible investment. His or her job is largely concerned with making life easier for you; taking phone messages, booking taxis, finding you somewhere to eat after the show, telling you when you have visitors and keeping them at bay when you don't want them. In the major subsidised companies like the RSC and the National, the more usual practice is to leave things till the end of the run, and then make a generous presentation of some sort.

You may also feel you'd like to show your appreciation to your dresser, for helping you with quick-changes, bringing you tea in the interval and going out to get you a sandwich between the shows. Dressers as a rule are appallingly badly paid, and a little something at the end of the week is generally much appreciated.

I sometimes feel inhibited about giving a gift of cash to someone who has come to be a close friend during our working relationship. I've found supermarket tokens a useful and acceptable alternative.

BRANCHING OUT

As time goes on, you may begin to feel that acting, by itself, doesn't completely satisfy your professional ambition; you have perhaps more to offer. We've talked about writing and teaching, but there may be other outlets for your talents.

Directing, for example. Sometimes as an actor you may have such a strong feeling for a play, and a conviction about how it should be interpreted, that even if there is no part in it for you, you still desperately want to say something about it.

Actors very often make good directors – they can see writing from the point of view of the characters rather than with a literary approach, and talk to actors in terms of what their character wants from a scene, rather than what they themselves want as director.

If you're planning to direct occasionally, whilst keeping acting as your main pursuit, you need to consider quite carefully how you mean to divide your time.

Directing a play involves a substantial period of lead-time, during which you will be involved in research, casting, talking to designers, attending production meetings and so on. None of this is paid for. What if your agent rings up and says, hey, there's this film in Naples, it just fits in, you'll fly home the day before you start rehearsal?

ORGANISATIONS AND CLUBS

Our profession is largely made up – as it should be – of what Dr Johnson termed 'clubbable people'. Clubs have always done well out of actors, but before you fill your notecase with a royal flush of brightly-coloured member-ship cards, ask yourself whether you'll find time to patronise them, or indeed whether you'll be able to afford the subscriptions year after year.

Perhaps you will. In that case, to have one informal club in central London where you can arrange to meet people, to have a snack or a drink, or simply sit down for a bit between interviews or before a show, is a useful extravagance. Health Clubs can be an economical way of using a gym regularly, and we've already talked about the Actors Centre.

Membership to the British Film Institute, if you live in or near London, is well worthwhile. If you become a Friend of the RSC, the National, the English National Opera or any of the dozens of other performing arts organisations, you will be entitled to occasional price concessions, priority booking and admission to various ancillary events.

COMMITTEE WORK

As time goes on, you may yourself be invited to join a number of different professional or quasi-professional organisations. Only do so if you feel that your presence may really assist their interests as well as your own, and that you honestly have the time to give them.

For example, a theatre company with whom you have been closely involved might ask you to join their governing body. There is often a shortage of practical experience on theatre boards, and the Artistic Director of the company may be very glad of your support at meetings.

The position is not salaried, of course. You will need to be a good diplomatist, to make your point across the table simply and clearly, to be able to read a balance sheet and to make sense of a mound of what may seem to you completely irrelevant paperwork. You also need to understand your individual financial responsibilities as a Board Member, which in times of adversity can have very serious implications.

And don't use board meetings as an opportunity to do some acting!

Current market philosophy has turned head teachers, vice chancellors, consultant surgeons and heads of law chambers into businessmen, and to some extent the same is true of us who feel concerned for the welfare of the theatrical profession. We sit on committees, become trustees, directors or governors, and of course ninety per cent of the time is taken up talking about money. Our involvement, our experience is, I believe, genuinely valuable, but we do have to be careful that these responsibilities don't begin to clog our own wheels, sap our energy and perhaps become an excuse for not having done something a bit more creative with the time. It's a matter of balance.

GIVING SOMETHING BACK

We work in the most widely spoken and understood language in the world, with probably the richest literary and dramatic heritage – I believe it's a moral and artistic duty to explore and promote it in any way possible. Unfortunately, that appears not to be a view shared by successive governments in this country, and it is therefore up to those of us who are directly involved to help how we can in saving endangered theatres, supporting theatrical charities, looking after elderly and disabled members of the profession, lobbying funding bodies and lending our name to various appeals.

Let's assume that you are in a situation of grateful solvency, and in a position to offer a helping hand to a deserving project, or person.

Actors, when they've been around for a while, tend to get a lot of requests from embryo production companies, organisers of arts events and, most frequently, drama students needing money for fees and maintenance.

Apart from those actually embarking on their training and seeking the means to do so, there are others already halfway through their courses who, having relied hitherto on financial support from their families, suddenly find that support collapsing owing to death of a parent, injury, redundancy, separation – and established members of the profession are often the easiest people to turn to in the emergency.

CHARITIES

You may also be deluged with requests from various charities. Choose *one*, or at the most two, that you really care about, to which you are prepared to give time as well as money, and with which you'd like to be identified, and politely refuse all others.

CELEBRITIES

We have been assuming that fortune has smiled on you, and that you are presently enjoying a degree of public success. Pru and I are delighted, and offer our warm congratulations. Watch out now for the first indication that you may find yourself described as a 'celebrity'. This dangerous appellation somehow suggests that this has now become your full-time job, and you must avoid it like the plague. If you think I'm being alarmist, look down any list of so-called 'celebrities' at a public function and ask yourself when the luminaries concerned last actually sang a song, kicked a football or presented a weather forecast.

Of course you will genuinely want to assist in the furtherance of causes that are dear to you, and if your name is identified in the public mind with integrity and fair-mindedness, it will be a useful addition to the list of supporters. When talking to the media about your interest, be aware that the press have a favourite way of trying to invalidate our views on any serious subject by dismissing us as 'luvvies' (an expression, incidentally, that I have never heard used by anyone in the business), concerned only with promoting our own achievements. I think we have a real responsibility to go on patiently trying to combat this.

WHEN TO STOP

Stopping is not a question of age: we can decide at any time that the life is not for us, that we are unable to make a living at it, that we quite simply don't enjoy it any more, and that we can withdraw gracefully without guilt, shame or apology.

Actors are fond of saying 'we never retire'; and in fact it's not we who retire, but the people who used to give us jobs, so it comes to the same thing really.

As one gets older, the range of parts naturally diminishes, and of course this has a disproportionate effect on women. In modern British drama there has always been – I don't know why – a lack of strong leading parts for women of 45 to 50. In Shakespeare, if you don't feel able still to cope with Cleopatra, there's Volumnia, Queen Margaret, Constance in *King John,* the Countess in *All's Well*, and that's about it.

In TV and film over the last couple of decades we've seen role models of both sexes getting younger and younger. Detective Inspectors used traditionally to be in their late forties; nowadays even Chief Superintendents are younger than that. The same is true for surgeons, barristers, head teachers and other genre-TV protagonists.

A disgruntled leading actress once told me she'd pack up and leave the business – if she thought anyone would notice. In fact she stayed, and went on to give, in a series of supporting parts, some of her best performances. To be constrained to cut one's coat, intricately, according to the available cloth is no bad thing.

As one gets older, the spectres of decreasing energy, physical ability, memory loss naturally start to loom, and a decision has to be made whether to ignore them, fight them, adapt, or capitulate.

Personally I want to die on the eighth curtain-call. The fact that there *were* eight would suggest the play is a success, and I'd hope to be somewhere near the middle of the line-up, having played a nice part reasonably well.

I've known older actors say, 'No, love, I don't do it anymore, can't remember the lines.' Certainly the learning does become more of a problem as one gets older, but there are usually ways of coping. Throughout your life I believe it's important to see as much new theatre, film and television as possible, so as to keep abreast of current techniques and usage; but then, one can often see older actors being *more* truthful or funny or powerful in modern productions than some of their younger colleagues, so – well, as I say, there is no reason to stop, *ever.*

APPENDIX

USEFUL PUBLICATIONS

Contacts, published annually by
Spotlight, 7 Leicester Place, London
WC2H 7RJ; t: 020 7437 7631;
e-mail: questions@spotlight.com;
www.spotlight.com
Copies (cost in 2014: £12.99 plus £3.21
p&p) can be ordered from the address
above or bought online. Essential for the
aspiring actor. Lists Agents; Casting
Directors; Drama Schools (and Coaches);
Film, TV and Radio Producers, Directors
and Executives; Photographers; Theatres
and Theatre Producers; and much more.

*Guide to Professional Training in Drama
and Technical Theatre,* published
annually by Drama UK (see below).

Spotlight, the essential casting directory
for the industry: five huge volumes of
actors and another five of actresses,
every entry consisting of a photo and
contact details. Their website explains
how you can appear in its pages, but
emphasises that '*Spotlight* only accepts
entries from artists who have recognised
training and/or professional acting
experience.' You can also search
Spotlight online for basic information
(see above).

The Stage, weekly newspaper containing news, reviews and job adverts for the acting profession. 47 Bermondsey Street, London SE1 3XT; t: 020 7403 1818; www.thestage.co.uk

Writers' and Artists' Yearbook, chiefly useful to actors for its lists of theatre producers (more selective and descriptive than that in *Contacts*) and of literary agents, who might be a source of reading work. Published annually (cost in 2014: £19.99) by Bloomsbury Publishing PLC, 50 Bedford Square, London WC1B 3DP; t: 020 7631 5600; e-mail: contact@bloomsbury.com; www.bloomsbury.com.

USEFUL ADDRESSES

The Actors Centre: a meeting place in Central London for professional actors to 'develop ideas, exchange information and support one another'. They run subsidised classes and have their own theatre, bar, restaurant and audition rooms. 1a Tower Street, Covent Garden, London WC2H 9NP; t: 020 7240 3940; e-mail: reception@actors.centre.co.uk

Actors' Church Union. St Paul's Church, Bedford Street, London WC2E 9Ed; t: 020 7836 5221; e-mail: info@actorschurch.org

BBC: Broadcasting House, Portland Place, London W1A 1AA; BBC Radio Drama: Room 6015, Broadcasting House, London W1A 1AA t: 020 7580 4468 www.bbc.co.uk

Drama UK (see Drama Training, below). Woburn House, 20 Tavistock Square, London WC1H 9HQ; t: 020 3393 6141 e-mail: info@dramauk.co.uk; www.dramauk.co.uk

Council for Dance Education and Training (CDET): does a similar job for dance training to what the Conference of Drama Schools does for drama training.
Old Brewer's Yard, 17-19 Neal Street, Covent Garden, London WC2H 9UY; t: 020 7240 5703;
e-mail: info@cdet.org.uk;
www.cdet.org.uk

Equity: the trade union for actors and performers. Guild House, Upper St Martin's Lane, London WC2H 9EG;
t: 020 7379 6000; e-mail: info@equity.org.uk; www.equity.org.uk

NODA (National Operatic and Dramatic Association): devoted to amateur theatre. 15 The Metro Centre, Peterborough, Cambridgeshire PE2 7UH;
t: 01733 374 790; e-mail: info@noda.org.uk; www.noda.org.uk

DRAMA TRAINING

Drama UK represents 20 of the UK's best-known drama training establishments (though many others are listed in *Contacts*). They are, in alphabetical order:

Academy of Live and Recorded Arts (ALRA) North and South

Arts Educational Schools London (ArtsEd)

Birmingham School of Acting

Bristol Old Vic Theatre School

Drama Centre London

Drama Studio London

East 15 London and East 15 Southend

GSA (Guildford School of Acting)

Guildhall School of Music and Drama

Italia Conti Academy of Theatre Arts

The Liverpool Institute for Performing Arts (LIPA)

The London Academy of Music and Dramatic Art (LAMDA)

Manchester Metropolitan University School of Theatre

Mountview Academy of Theatre Arts

The Oxford School of Drama

Rose Bruford College

Royal Academy of Dramatic Art (RADA)

The Royal Central School of Speech and Drama

Drama UK operates a useful website – www.dramauk.co.uk – which provides links to all the above schools and where you can read and download Drama UK's guide to all available accredited courses, as well as search for courses and, crucially, funding.

AGENTS

Contacts (see Publications, above) lists over 500 agents and personal managers of all sizes and specialities from the one-man band to the corporate agency. Those that are members of the professional body, the Personal Managers' Association (PMA), are asterisked.

PHOTOGRAPHERS

Again *Contacts* (see Publications, above) has a list of professional photographers, but only of those who have paid to advertise, though this does give you an opportunity to see their work – and their clients.

THEATRE BOOKS
MENTIONED IN THE TEXT

Uta Hagen with Haskel Frankel *Respect for Acting* (Macmillan, USA/UK 1973)

Uta Hagen *A Challenge for the Actor* (Scribner's, USA 1991)

Richard Hornby *The End of Acting - A Radical View* (Applause, USA 1994)

Litz Pisk *The Actor and His Body* (Methuen, UK 2003)

Athene Seyler *The Craft of Comedy* (Routledge, USA 1998)

Antony Sher *Beside Myself* (Arrow, UK 2002)

Publication details are of the latest known edition: you can sometimes get second-hand copies on Amazon.co.uk or Amazon.com.